Sandsanal 3.79
KAPGS
36×48"
#5-8226 Remiale

master @pr4

"DAYCLOSE" 4×
6 8115

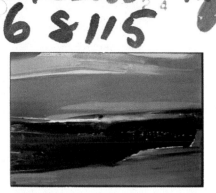

Nora Howard
·81

MARCH 1987 PHOTOCO

27

33

19 15·II·79
#230
RT.

+10

CHARLES SCHORRE
SEPT. 83
PHOTO ACRYLIC OIL
COLLAGE ON PAPER
83·P

22×14½

"PAGES FROM BOOKS
UNPUBLISHED"
5

NOV 1982 8219 1
PHOTO CO.
"WINGED MONUMENT"

36 ×48
ACRYLIC, OIL, CANVAS

22 NOV. 1987 PHOTOCO

18 (455) 31"×22½"

DEC. 1988 PHOTOCO

OIL ACRYLIC PHOTO COLLAGE ON PAPER

"DEVIL'S DOOR"
3 2 O 5 5

6·8/80 27

NOV 1982 8244 15
PHOTO CO.

STARROMANCING
SEPT. 1988 PHOTOCO

LORIE 3187

3½×24¾
19

OR 18

SEASIGNAL · 1·79   36×44
#5-8280

392

136 Sec.

Nora Howard '81

163) CHARLES SCHORRE
2406 TANGLEY
HOUSTON, TX. 77005

#6·8026   1·80
"Seasignal"
36×48"

360

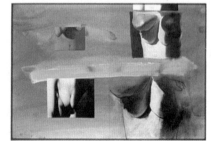

PHOTO, OIL, ACRYLIC
PAPER COLLAGE
22×29

Vedette Oil Co. '80

372

175   IVAN 53
Charles Schorre 2406

363 375 GLOVER

Charles Schorre

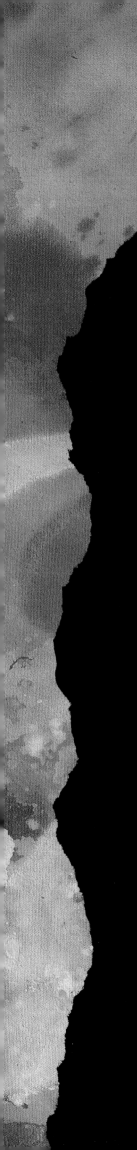

Charles Schorr

Edited and designed by Jerry Herrin

Introduction by Anne Wilkes Tucke

Essay by Jim Edwards

Exhibition curated by David E. Brau

Major photography by Rick Gardne

Additional text by Geoff Winningha
Ivan Chermayeff, James Bell and Le
Thomas, Carol Everingham, Dugald
Stermer, Patricia C. Johnson, Norma
Kent, and Dave Crossley

Published by Herring Press and
the Houston Artists Fund

1997

Charles Schorre left a lasting impression on the people who met him, who were taught by him, who own his work, and even those with only a passing interest in what he created. This book is a result of his influence.

In the spring of 1994, a conversation between Lomis Slaughter and Alexander McLanahan about Schorre, his studio and his work, started the ball rolling. A group of people who have followed Schorre's life journey gathered together and set about to support the mounting of a major exhibition of his work. This book is a companion to that effort and is being published to coincide with the 1997 opening of the Charles Schorre exhibition at the Art Museum of South Texas in Corpus Christi.

The Charles Schorre Project, sponsored by the Houston Artists Fund, consists of an advisory board that includes Alexander K. McLanahan (chairman), Lomis Slaughter (treasurer), John Boehm, Betty Fleming, Frederic Fleming, Lester Giese, Jane H. Gregory, Helen S. Morgan, Alton Z. Parks, Jr., and Wallace S. Wilson.

Charles Schorre died while this book was being created. The project was brought to fruition with the help and guidance of his loving — and loved — wife, Miggie.

The Influence of a Gentle Man   A tall man with his arms across his chest, standing to the side in a crowded room, Charles Schorre did nothing to attract my attention. But I felt his keen observation. If I looked up and caught his eye, he smiled. Such a lovely smile. The formidable intensity of a prior moment disappeared into ripples of wrinkles. That's my first, and forever, memory of Charles Schorre (who was known as Charlie to his closest friends and relatives).

When he was working — sketching, painting, photographing, making collages, or exchanging ideas — his expression could be fierce. If you fawned, tried to box him in a corner, or otherwise displeased him, he glowered. But if he liked you, he was charming in a very quiet way. He was quick to compliment, solicitous of your health, and a good listener. A lot of people liked and respected him, people of very different professions, incomes, and ages. They encompassed the many different aspects of his careers and interests. He won medals in art direction, editorial illustration, and graphic design. He was a good

Schorre posed for photographer Rick Gardner in his Houston studio on Morningside.

teacher in both accredited classes and spontaneous sidewalk discussions. At biannual intervals, he exhibited his wildly joyous paintings and watercolors. He published small books of his drawings and photographs. He seriously adored his family.

Reading reviews of his exhibitions is a bit of a love feast. In 1976, Mimi Crossley noted "what a superb craftsman and draftsman he is," adding that his "collages are some of the best work produced in Houston this season." Two years later, Charlotte Moser observed that at 53 Schorre was "a generation older than the young artists for which Houston is known. Yet his outlook remains perennially contemporary." Carol Everingham pronounced him to be "a master of the uninhibited line." Susie Kalil also commented on Schorre's ability to remain "free of inhibitions and full of childish wonder." Therefore, she continued, "the work [is] always renewing itself and consistently putting to use in some manner all of his artistic faculties." In 1981, Patricia Johnson was also struck by Schorre's sense of play and

A portrait by Schorre of his wife, Miggie, taken while on a trip to Santa Fe.

wonder. Her review began: "Sometimes sensual, sometimes formal, Charles Schorre's *Pages From Books Unpublished* dances across the walls of the Contemporary Arts Museum." Fourteen years later, she reported that he continued "to explore the magic of pure color in his recent paintings on canvas and paper. . . and the energy and assurance of his brush strokes have not dimmed." Throughout his career, art critics have used words such as joy, skill, spontaneity, content, screams and whispers. High praise indeed.

Beyond the praise for his art, there are the testaments to his capacity as a teacher. First from 1948 to 1955 at the Museum of Fine Arts School (now the Glassell School of Art), then in the School of Architecture at Rice University from 1960 to 1972, he goaded, teased, and inspired with his own example and his capacity to philosophize through apt analogies. Schorre's old friend and colleague E.M. "Buck" Schiwetz reported returning to his studio "with new vigor" after sitting in some of Schorre's summer workshops. Peers in the graphic arts similarly

A self-portrait, taken in the 1960s while at the Kelvin Group studios. Schorre needed a portrait for a magazine article, so he framed himself among photographs of the women in his life: his wife, Miggie, in the lower left and his three daughters across the top.

remember being energized by casual contact with him. Years after taking his classes, students brought portfolios by his studio and invited him to their exhibitions. Schorre himself described his pedagogic method as asking questions and sharing a course of discovery with his students. Like any good teacher, he professed to learn more than he taught. He compared his approach to that of Marcel Duchamp who asked a student, "What are you doing?" The student said, "I don't know," and Duchamp said, "Good, keep it up." For Schorre, it was a search, not an arrival, that most interested him, and this kept him mentally young and his art vigorous.

I don't mean to imply that Charles didn't have detractors, maybe even enemies. He was human, very human. It was part of his understanding of the human condition to which he professed deepest allegiance. Into his paintings he unabashedly poured feelings honed by years of observations—made standing in rooms with his arms crossed.

— Anne Wilkes Tucker *Gus and Lyndall Wortham Curator, Museum of Fine Arts, Houston*

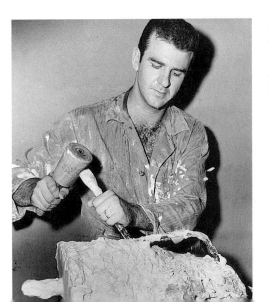

Sculpting while a teacher at the Museum of Fine Arts, Houston, in 1950.

The Studio

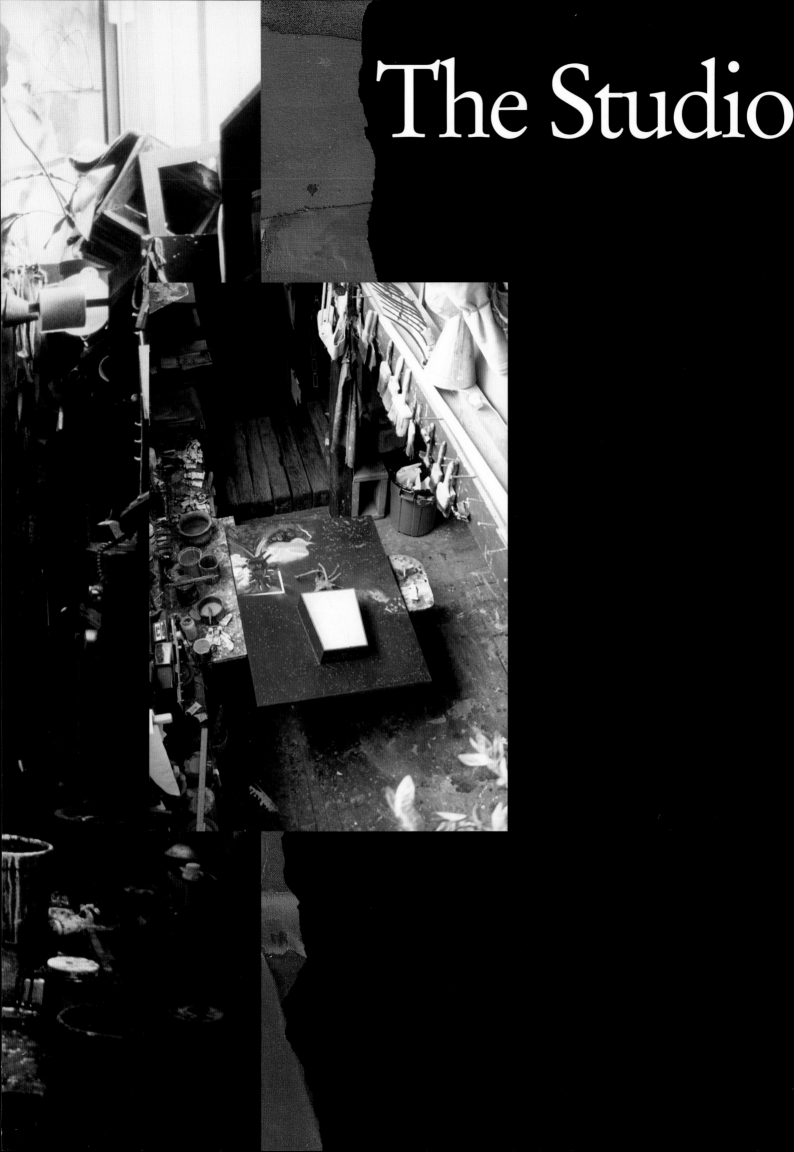

Charlie's work flowed out of him in so many conscious and unconscious ways. He managed to get most of it down on paper or canvas, but what didn't make it ended up scattered around him in his studio. Because the colors and gestures that he sent off could not be held by the canvases laid out in front of him, it seemed as if the walls of his small, two-and-a-half-room work space were coated with the energy of his mind. His work had always been a combination of thought and play, adventure and cunning. And beyond the edges of his canvases, in the shelves and nooks and crannies of his studio, were vignettes of these activities: notes and sketches, objects set artfully against one another, letters from acquaintances ready to be responded to, and the tools of his trade. . . ordinary objects all, but here in the light of this place, special. The aura of Charlie's small studio cannot be overplayed. It is not sentimentality that makes for such fond memories of the place; it was, in fact, an environment that evoked a sense of awe from its visitors, a feeling of excitement and wonder. Thousands of surfaces were crammed into the nearly suffocating space, and each surface reflected vibrant shapes and color or

Left, above: Schorre in the doorway of his Morningside studio, photographed by Rick Gardner in 1969. The small studio is in the converted garage of a house in the Rice University Village area of Houston. Schorre rented the rooms of the house as studios for illustrators, photographers, designers, and architects before moving his residence there in 1982. Left, below: the office area of Schorre's studio.

presented a deep, purplish black recess that served as a backdrop for the color dancing around the room. This was Charlie's sacred place, full of his sounds, his activities. Full of his projects, sometimes four to six works moving along at the same time. He liked it that way. . . changing from one piece to another, letting his mind wander, letting his art take him places. He could be distracted by little nuances, what we would call day-dreaming. Or he could become so intent that he would ignore other activities and concerns. I very much liked visiting Charlie in this place. Because when I left, I would feel rejuvenated, fresh. That is the effect this place had, this small, cramped inferno of spontaneity. This work in progress. —Jerry Herring

Above: the stairway to the loft. Right, above: a wall adorned with birds' nests, honeycombs, and hand-painted pots. Right, below: a view into one of the studio's several work areas.

Left: a view into Schorre's primary painting area. Above: two views of Schorre at the Kelvin Group in the early 1960s. Before having his own studio on Morningside, Schorre worked at the Kelvin Group studios, primarily as an illustrator. It was there, however, that he began his Emerge series.

Left and right, above: portraits of Schorre just after moving into his new space on Morningside in 1969. Rick Gardner's photos capture the studio in an earlier, more ordered, time. The walls would become more and more layered, reflecting Schorre's energetic output.

Page 25

Charles Schorre: Polarities and their goodness

> "There was a purpose
> and a plan. . .
> Then you throw the plan away
> and improvise as best you can
> to accomplish original purpose
> . . .and sometimes this purpose
> gets bent in the <u>process</u>
> which becomes the purpose."
> 4 May '79[1]

Charles Schorre was born in Cuero, Texas, in 1925. In 1948, the same year he married Margaret Storm, he moved to Houston to work for the advertising agency of Foote, Cone & Belding. If we include his student days at the University of Texas (1946-1948), then Schorre spent 50 of his 71 years as an artist. He died in July 1996 in Houston, Texas. His was a remarkable career in many ways, beginning just as the post-World War II impact of regionalism was being challenged by modernism and abstract expressionism, the school of abstraction being practiced in New York. Very early in his career, Schorre made a decision to go his own way, to stay interested in many things, and to develop a career as an artist that was a natural avocation of his living rather than an occupation that was specialized, and somehow separate, from other aspects of his life. He worked to the very last days of his life, and what he left behind in the Houston studio that he occupied for 35 years is an amazing archive of paintings, graphics, photographs, daybooks, art materials, rocks, nests, letters, slides, art and photography books, etc., all the materials and souvenirs of a life creatively lived.

By the late 1940s and early 1950s, Schorre had begun to produce prints and paintings depicting a semiabstract crucifix, a compositional T-shape with Christ's bowed head seen from slightly above, his extended body and legs forming a vertical line down the middle of the canvas or paper, and his outstretched arms forming a horizontal band near the top of the composition. These early crucifix paintings cast Schorre as a religious painter, an odd position to be in during an era when the prevailing mode in the art world was secular and/or existential. Later, in 1964 on the occasion of the Rice University exhibition *Charles Schorre: Cruciforms*, the artist acknowledged that religious painting at the time had no authority with the media and, with great wit, indicated that "if this historical happening is your only religious experience, you can't be blamed if someone 'proves' that it didn't happen. You can't be blamed for not having the guts to have your own religious experience. You might be afraid that it might be 'out' or 'camp,' the wrong thing to do that year, just as Christ's being on the cross was the wrong thing to do that other year."[2]

As Schorre further abstracted these cruciform works, they became known as the *Emerge* series, typified by the small oil on linen *Emerge I* (1959). In the numerous drawings and paintings of this series, the cruciform began to not only represent Christ on the cross but also be seen as a bird with spreading wings, a butterfly, a vagina, a heart, etc. Schorre also began observing the transformational qualities of these cruciforms in nature — in shells, for instance, or in the prints left in the sand by

---

[1]This quote was found in a daybook that was a journal Schorre kept for his 1979 trip to Saudi Arabia as an Artist-in-Residence sponsored by Mobil Corporation, 1979.

[2]Charles Schorre, quoted in Dugald Stermer, "Charles Schorre," *Communication Arts Magazine*, vol. 9, no. 2, 1967, p. 73.

seabirds. What he was recognizing within and outside of the religious connotations of the cruciform was nature's own organic life patterns and the birth-life-death cycle that it came to represent. The cruciform would continue to inform Schorre's art his whole life, right up to his last exhibition, *Charles Schorre: Recent Paintings*, which was held at Meredith Long & Company in the winter of 1995. On the invitation for that exhibition was a color reproduction of the five-foot-square oil painting *Tri-Emerge (1993)*, with the cruciform now presented as a triptych. After years of working with single or diptych formats, Schorre had begun adopting the new configuration of the triptych, one whose form suggests the Holy Trinity of Christianity.

Over the course of his career, Schorre became a bolder and more confident painter. He began experimenting with various spontaneous working procedures, exercising less control over his application of paint by pouring it or using it to stain the canvas. For a 1978 exhibition of Schorre's paintings, Ian Glennie described the artist's painting process: "... The painted 'ground' layer of the canvas is composed of controlled accidents arising from manipulation of the canvas and the sequential application of successive layers of various pure colors. The canvas is manipulated by crumpling. . . . The crumpling of the fabric allows the successive layers of paint to puddle and mix, producing an almost geomorphic surface."[3] After achieving this colored ground, Schorre would often next superimpose calligraphic markings. By these processes, he was moving away from the more traditional demands of figurative illustration, which involves first defining a form by outlining, then filling in the drawn form with color. Schorre, in fact, reversed this procedure by activating the surface of the painting with a flood of color, applied independently of any representational description or sense of volume by illusionistic shading, then allowing the superimposed drawing not to add definition of form to color so much as to act as accent or counterpoint. The tension created between the colored surface and the linear elements works against the deep space of Renaissance perspective and creates instead a figure/ground relationship that is more shallow, transparent, interchangeable, and metaphorically suggestive. In the chromatically hot painting *Touchrush* (1973), Schorre flooded the canvas surface with intense hues: ultramarines, cobalts, and cadmium reds and yellows, which bled

[3]Ian Glennie, *Charles Schorre: Recent Works*, brochure (College Station: Texas A&M University, 1978), unpaginated.

Previous, page 26: **Self Portrait** *ND. Watercolor, 9½ x 7½ inches. Artist's Collection.*

Above: **Cruciform 81** *1964. Oil on canvas, 40 x 48 inches. Lomis Slaughter Collection.*

to violets and oranges as they mixed on the canvas. The intensity of these pure colors is further agitated by the white, pink, and yellow calligraphic lines that weave in and out of the pooled colors or lie on top.

Schorre seemed to have no fear that these intensely blazoned paintings would become overly riotous or decorative. He acknowledged the danger, however, saying "it is very risky for me to be colorful. . . like it is difficult in our time to paint a truly fine sunset."[4] The tension of polarities that exists in the conflict of color and line kept Schorre's paintings in a tug-of-war between his love for color and his great skills as a draftsman. This battle also kept his work on canvas and work on paper very closely related to one another and, in some of his best work, even commingling in the form of collage. The drawn or painted line was perhaps his first impulse, but the sense of texture and emotion that color supplied did not so much divide his attention as it allowed him another ingredient for immediacy.

In his statement for the catalogue of The Museum of Fine Arts, Houston, *Fresh Paint* exhibition, Schorre acknowledged his sources of inspiration: "I consider nature to be my most important influence and source. Natural lines, colors, smells, natural currents such as desert sandstorms, rainstorms, stillness, anything unadorned, without fashion — old rocks, new buildings before they are dressed up, naked ladies, fossils, shells, clouds, dirt."[5] Taking nature as a teacher, Schorre remained sensitive all his life to its forms and its patterns of movement. The work of a brilliant draftsman, Schorre's drawings attempt not only to render a form but also to capture its sense of growth and movement. His contour lines both describe, for instance, the circumference of a flower and suggest the plant's reaching and unfolding towards its source of nourishment, the sun, or its bending to the power of the wind. The act of drawing was much more than just a skill acquired for describing a subject. For Schorre, drawing was the act that best exercised his working imagination; it's what he did best and what I suspect he loved to do the most. The manner in which he often approached other media, such as painting and photography, had about it a sense of intuition and spontaneity that we often identify with the art of drawing. His photographs of the female nude depict the model leaning, bending, or twisting, the impulse being towards motion rather than repose.

The opportunity to see beyond surface detail was

[4]Charles Schorre, *Drawings & Notes* (Houston: Seashore Press, 1975), unpaginated.

[5]Charles Schorre, quoted in Barbara Rose and Susie Kalil, *Fresh Paint: The Houston School*, exh. cat. (Austin: Texas Monthly Press, 1985), p. 168.

Touchrush *1973. Acrylic on canvas, 60 x 96 inches. Frederic and Betty Fleming Collection.*

Page 29

always a goal of his mark and picture making. Drawing and photography certainly allowed Schorre the leisure to explore the surfaces of his subjects, while also underlining that reality was what he called "This other 'presence'. . . the visual essence, trace or residue. . . and this visual residue, if it can be produced graphically, is what I like to think of as my drawings."[6] What Schorre described also suggests a state of automatism, and here I am thinking not of the psychic automatism practiced by the surrealists, whose aim was to bring the workings of the subconscious graphically to the forefront, but rather a free form of drawing after nature, a reinterpretation of the seen and felt where the seeing and the feeling as content become inseparable from the forms depicted. This constant desire on Schorre's part to meld observation and response gives his drawings an extraordinary vitality and immediacy. In his masterful little book *Drawings & Notes II,* we can see what great range and variety he could achieve in the quick sketch, from the landscape notations of the Guadalupe River and Big Bend in Texas and of his travels in Saudi Arabia to the pure fantasy of his "Bone" drawings.

Although the quick sketch and contour drawings, of which he did thousands in his notebooks, will probably never be considered as important as his paintings and photo-collages, I believe they represent Schorre at his finest. He was not an artist who sought the heraldic image as a symbol for the heroic moment; even in his early more representational and ironic *Emerge* series, the image tends to show Christ as if he were about to slide or fly off the cross or, in the more abstract versions, going through some kind of transformation. Schorre's years as a graphic illustrator had challenged him to take any moment, no matter how mundane, and to infuse it with life through line, color, and form. His own predilection to follow closely the world about him, whether his subjects of south Texas or his travels, was enough to stimulate his full attention. His attention was, in fact, not that of someone making calculated moves on the art world but rather that of a witness to the life about him; as he has said, "I can only respond as an artist to what I *SEE* and what *MY HISTORY* brings to this."[7]

His act of seeing was not a static one. As an afterword to Schorre's beautifully designed book *Drawings and Notes II*, Susie Kalil wrote, ". . . it can be said that the artist sets up equivalents, where a

[6]Charles Schorre, *Drawings & Notes* (Houston: Seashore Press, 1975), unpaginated.

[7]Charles Schorre, *Drawings & Notes* (Houston: Seashore Press, 1975), unpaginated.

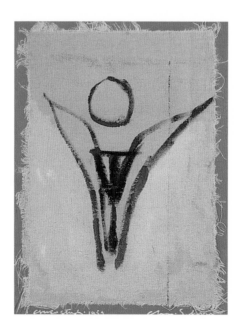

Emerge I *1959. Oil on linen mounted on board, 12 x 9 inches. Artist's Collection.*

single line serves commensurately a torso, a shell, cloud or rock formation. Yet the artist's penchant for employing cross-references within his own body of work is not a calculated measure inasmuch as an afterthought and outgrowth of loosely connected accidents. The abstracted image in a recent work called *Insect Song* looks strangely similar to the cruciform painted nearly thirty years ago. A photograph taken some seven years ago of an abalone shell evinces spirals and radiating lines comparable to those employed in the 'Bone' drawings."[8] For Schorre, the recycling and metamorphosis of known forms provided a path for him to resee and renew. At the most heightened state of chance or accident, whether poured paint or freely drawn quick sketch, the paint or pencil often seemed to have a mind of its own.

Schorre's mastery of the quick sketch was both a strength and a weakness. The spontaneous gesture gave his work a marvelous quivering energy, but it also, like so many techniques of automatism, gave his compositions and subjects an ephemeral look, as though they were about to rush off to the next idea or activity. Like the abstract expressionists familiar to him from his early years, Schorre's faith in the

creative act itself was more important to him than the art object itself. Process, rather than product, was what really interested him. He claimed, in fact, like Alberto Giacometti never to have finished anything except his commercial work as a graphic designer. Schorre's belief in this principle of art was reinforced by the notion that life and art are dynamic processes and that observation and invitation should not be separate from execution. Believing this, the artist can be thought of as some kind of conduit, a participant who, if quick of eye and hand, can follow the natural movements to the birth of a form instead of simply rendering a form after the fact of its coming into existence. Here, the stress is placed on the creation rather than the "finish" or completion of a form.

In 1977, Schorre began a series of collages that was to occupy him for the rest of his life. Known as *Pages From Books Unpublished*, the works represent a summation of Schorre's lifetime concerns. Even the title of this series alludes to a state of being unfinished, ongoing, and perhaps never-ending. These collages are filled with references to landscape, architecture, and the human body. Essentially mixed media works on paper, they were often presented as

[8]Susie Kalil, afterword, in Charles Schorre, *Drawings & Notes II* (Houston: Seashore Press, 1983), unpaginated.

Untitled *1975. Ink on paper (line drawing from* Drawings & Notes*), 4 x 5¼ inches. Artist's Collection.*

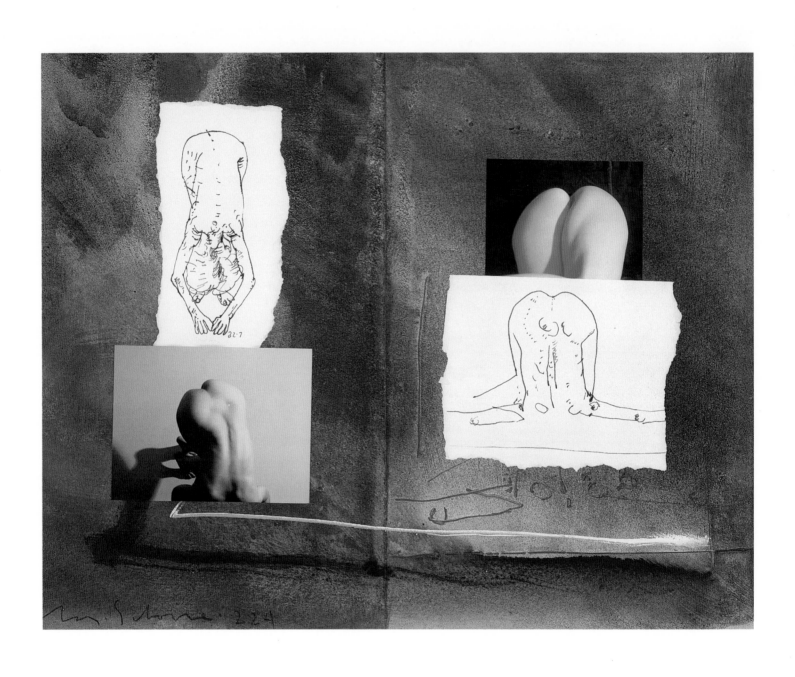

Pages From Books Unpublished #224 *ND. Mixed-media collage on paper, 22½ x 30 inches. Private Collection.*

diptychs and incorporate all manner of media: acrylic and oil paint, pencil, charcoal, watercolor, and photography. Unlike most collagists, who tend to use found printed matter, Schorre used only his own material, whether drawings from his notebooks or his own photography of nature and the female nude. Because of his liberal use of photographs, works in *Pages From Books Unpublished* are often referred to as photo-collages.

Schorre appears to have devoted only the minimum amount of preplanning to his "pages." They naturally fall into subject groupings, the earliest works in a group being more realistic and narrative and the later ones more abstract and poetic, but the collages also took up issues that Schorre was exploring independently in his paintings, as he had hinted in his notebooks. The very early collage #2 (1977) is a diptych on a horizontal format that is dense with information: figures and portraits, drawings, detailed notes of trips taken and things seen, small reproductions and drawings of his own paintings, photographs from his series *The Artist's Handbook*, etc. Somewhere near the middle of the series comes #224 (ND), a diptych also measuring 22½ x 30 inches but having a more simplified composition: two line drawings and two photographs are juxtaposed, showing a model bending over, her back and raised buttocks facing us. Schorre would often lightly spray paint at an angle across the support papers backing the collages, giving the backgrounds the misty, damp look of watercolor or washy acrylic.

When the *Pages From Books Unpublished* collages were first exhibited in 1981 at the CEPA Gallery in Buffalo, New York, and then in Houston at the Contemporary Arts Museum, they drew positive attention. But in otherwise praiseworthy reviews, Mimi Crossley wrote, ". . . the series is highly accomplished, even elegant, but ultimately too predictable,"[9] and Patricia Johnson, who championed Schorre's work throughout his life, observed, ". . . they obviously have great importance to Schorre's growth as a fine artist. Nevertheless, they are minor when compared to his paintings."[10] At the time, both critics were most likely correct in their judgments; even an exhibition of 34 of these early collages, each

dealing with subtle variations of a similar subject, could not provide a broad enough view of where the artist was headed. But by his winter 1988 exhibition at Houston's Meredith Long gallery, Schorre's *Pages* series had reached more than 400 collages with the range of subjects, color, and manners of execution vastly expanded.

The collage process that guided *Pages From Books Unpublished* was ideally suited to Schorre's temperament as an artist. It allowed him to work through ideas that were based upon principles of analogy and to express feelings and forms that were suggestive as well as descriptive. In this mode, Schorre's collages can be thought of as a kind of visual poetry. Collage, as Schorre practiced it, was also important experientially for its intimate and informal values, more tactile in its cutting, tearing, placing, and gluing than is usually allowed in painting (though Schorre would often add torn and painted strips of canvas to his paintings). Collage can also, as Dore Ashton has said of Robert Motherwell, function like a journal: ". . . it is as wide-ranging as the spirit, which flows on, unperturbed, as the mundane events of a day mark off real time, sometimes it is built upon a visual pleasure. . . sometimes it is built upon a fragment of a thought. . . , sometimes it is built upon a fusion of intellectual and sensuous encounter. . . ."[11] Ashton's definition of Motherwell's collage process could apply equally to Schorre, and it was Motherwell, especially as a collagist, of all the New York School artists who had developed out of modernism that the Houston artist related most closely to.

There was for Schorre an organic working process in the making of his photo-collages, what must have seemed like a dance in slow motion with sudden bursts of creativity, a sequence of moments of recognition and surprise: a torn piece of discarded collage material accidentally leaning against a painting of ten years ago or a daybook with sketches of cloud formations found sitting on top of some recent photographic proof sheets, etc. As these fragments of daily life found their way into his collage making, the most important thing was to allow metaphors to appear naturally out of Schorre's keen attention and with the materials at hand. And for metaphors to

[9]Mimi Crossley, "Schorre: Pages From Books Unpublished," *The Houston Post*, July 3, 1981.

[10]Patricia C. Johnson, "'Pages' Utilizes Schorre's Interests in Dual Media," *Houston Chronicle*, July 3, 1981, sec. 4, p. 10.
[11]Dore Ashton, "Robert Motherwell: The Painter and His Poets," in H. H. Arnason, *Robert Motherwell* (New York: Abrams, 1982), p. 8.

appear naturally and to end up in collages takes time. As Schorre so poetically described the process, ". . . I make a mark and hope that mark reactivates a response, I respond, the marks respond, my move, your move, etc., etc."[12]

We are perhaps too close to Schorre's recent death to take a long critical view of his life's work. As an influential graphic designer and a much admired teacher in the School of Architecture at Rice University, Schorre won the admiration of many. He can easily be placed in the first generation of Houston artists, as David Brauer did in his 1993 Glassell School of Art exhibition *Artist's Progress, Seven Houston Artists* 1943-1993, where Schorre was joined by Harvey Bott, Jack Boynton, Don Foster, Dorothy Hood, Don Shaw, and Dick Wray. Nonetheless, there seems to be no "Charles Schorre look-alikes" pressing their way onto the marketplace. Schorre inspired by example, not by style or as an advocate of some particular school or "ism." His work was too self-referential and free of inhibitions to be easily "stylized" into a look that could be passed on to others. His art reveals a man who was essentially a loner, drawing heavily upon his own love of nature and mark making.

As for those artists who influenced him, there were many. Schorre enjoyed an acquaintance and friendships with many artists, both famous and unknown, including Motherwell; he was especially close to the photographer Aaron Siskind. Of the artists that Schorre admired from art history, he paid tribute to many by including reproductions of their paintings and drawings in his collages and further honoring them by naming the works after them: *Degasspirit, Matissespirit, Manetspirit,* etc. He loved Rodin, Picasso, Klee, and all the great draftsmen of modernism. At times a particular work by Schorre will contain a form or a series of marks that suggests another's work. For instance, in Schorre's 1983 painting *I Cross My Heart and Hope To. . .,* the loosely drawn heart shapes come from the buttocks of a female model that he drew and photographed in life class, but they also strongly resemble the sketchy valentine shapes that the late Los Angeles artist John Altoon once used in a series of ink and pastel draw-

ings of the mid 1960s. The fluid spread and intensely bold hues of some of Schorre's landscape watercolors at times exhibit a color and form sense that is closely related to work by the New Mexico watercolorist Keith Crown. Where they differ fundamentally is that Altoon's work is more tragicomic in tone and Crown's is more cubist in design. But in all cases these resemblances are a likeness and not a "group think" aesthetic dictating a particular look.

It is my sense that there are no singular "masterpieces" in Schorre's production. His art was not progressively developmental in a way that would allow for a *Guernica* to emerge, nor was Schorre's career pointed towards a historically defining moment. What Charles Schorre did leave us was a large body of resolved work that was built on the premise of the creative act as an effort to join a very individualized moment of intuition with one of execution. From his notes on his trip to Saudi Arabia in 1979, which recorded both the beauty (desert landscape and architecture) and the horrors (dead camels and officious bureaucrats) of this ancient land, he had written, ". . . I've always believed in the existence of polarities and their goodness."[13]

Schorre was an extraordinarily honest man. He had a large appetite for beauty and truth, which made him at times appear to be a "religious painter" and at other times appear decidedly romantic. He also had developed over time a marvelous sense of the syncopation of metaphors of the visual world: how dissimilar objects can share a form or a color. (How a woman's buttocks can resemble the shape of a valentine heart or spilled red paint may suggest a setting sun.) He trusted the paradox of metaphor, like the classic form of the Japanese haiku where nature's seemingly eternal beauty is held next to a sense of humankind's fleeting, mortal presence. For Schorre it was not the one thing alone that attracted his attention but the fact that more than one idea could coexist in the same composition. It was at the moment of tension in polarities that Charles Schorre produced his most vivid juxtapositions whose drawn or painted shapes were quickly rendered and whose impulse as visual residue was joyous in spirit.

—Jim Edwards

[12]Charles Schorre, *Drawings & Notes* (Houston: Seashore Press, 1975), unpaginated.
[13]From notes found in Schorre's handwriting on the back of an exhibition announcement.

Life Class

9/24/66
First class day am
Semester final:class profile that is to start immediately

prang watercolor set

Paper due in one hour: who are you
    due next class   what are you doing here?
                  where have you been?
                  What is the most meaningful(traumatic) thing
                    that ever happened to you?
                  3 most important movies
                  3 most important indutrial designers
                  " " "   graphic designers
                  " " "   painters & sculptors & etc.
                  " " "   musicians or composers (jazz or
                  " " "   authors or books
                  Don't bore me but tell me about you
                  Where will you be five years from now and what
                    will you be doing?
                  Where would you really like to be five years
                    from now and what would you really like
                    to be doing?
                  List some other main interests
                  What do you expect from me and this class?

...more about class profile...content,concept,originality of presenta-
    tion...these things most important...next and if it is a fine
    contributive piece of work...is it publishable...as is...Mr.
    Caudill's Rice triad (Design Technology Management)...when you
    are finished, it should have involved all of these things.

pm/draw naked girl sitting in chair with stuffed owl in her lap

...on any first rainy day we will work in the studio with our
watercolor sets...all drawing and painting the same old house

ps:who are the good photographers in this class, who has a station
   wagon???
   How many could spare a Thursday evening instead of some afternoon
   How many could pick up and go to Galveston?
     //...if so who will volunteer to plan etc for trip...food and
      everthing.

                                9-12 LIF
CLASS NEXT WEEK(if a pretty sunny day) will be spent at the zoo 1 PM
        ...we can even eat there if you want ...watercolor...
        drawing ...photoing...writing...rose garden...trees
        at the museum of Burke Baker.

NEXT THURS. 9-12 1-5 LIFE

Charles Schorre, teacher. For thirteen years, from 1959 until 1972, Schorre taught life drawing to students in the School of Architecture at Rice University. Initially invited to teach architecture students the skills to render people, trees, and automobiles, Schorre molded a more varied curriculum that included poetry, music, photography, and life drawing. Schorre's very popular class inspired a generation of architects and would-be architects who became writers, photographers, and other inhabitants of the art and business worlds. Schorre took his life class on investigative journeys through form, line, weight, color. . . passion, sight, and awareness in the classrooms at Rice, on the campus lawn, and among downtown skyscrapers. Schorre: "Each one of us is a unique contraption (piece of architecture). Our fathers and mothers made us so. Therefore, our traces (marks, scratchings, architecture) should be so."

Left: a student drawing from Schorre's life drawing class. Left, inset: Schorre's typewritten notes for his class in 1966. Above: Schorre sketches a figure for his attentive students. Following pages: a student photograph of the life drawing class on the lawn at Rice University. Following pages, inset: a typical year-end portrait of Schorre and his class.

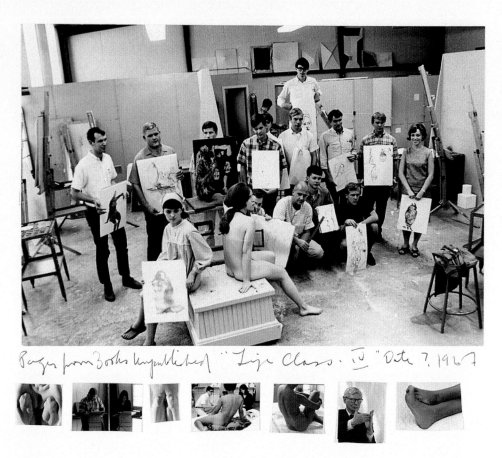

Pages from Books Unpublished "Life Class. IV" Date 7, 1967

+12QG53456JG78970+RGG512+3+4NEG516171819 RG1920212BG23 24 252GRG27

Pages from Books Unpublished "Life Class IV" Nancy Graham

11 Nov 69

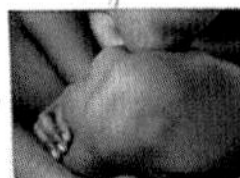

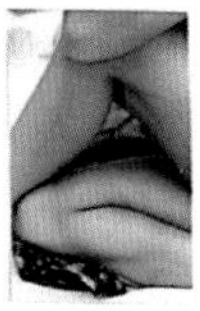

I remember Charles Schorre as perhaps the most passionate artist and teacher I've ever known. He literally crackled with ideas and energy. I cannot remember him sitting still or stopping for any period of time to consider his next move. He just *did* things. He drew and painted and ripped up photos for collage in the same way he conducted class: passionately.

I had just received my bachelor's degree from Rice — in English, never having taken an art course of any kind — when I walked into the first session of Schorre's drawing and watercolor class in the fall of 1965. I had deferred my admission to law school for a year to test my late-blooming interest in photography. I had been told that Schorre knew a good bit about photography and welcomed students of diverse artistic interests into his class.

The first class encompassed a rambling monologue by Schorre on the importance of "staying loose" and a showing of some of his recent drawings, paintings, and collages. He concluded by giving an assignment, due in two days, to draw something, anything at all, and bring it to the next class. He wanted to see our own choice of subject and our natural way of drawing before he offered any advice.

I had never attempted to draw in my life, and I felt intimidated by the other students, mostly architects, who seemed much more prepared for this class than I.

Nevertheless, I remember that I did a series of small drawings on one sheet of paper. Schorre had urged us to draw without inhibition or preconception. To be natural. To draw what we like to look at. So I made a childlike attempt at sketching various animals at the zoo.

In the next class, Schorre had us all hang our work on the wall, and he went from piece to piece, commenting. When he came to my little series of sketches, he stopped and looked for a few seconds. "Whose is this?" he asked. I owned up. He looked at me for an instant, then back at the drawings. "Can you use a camera, do you know how to take photographs?" Several in the class laughed, well aware already of my photography skills.

"Then stop trying to draw," he said. "You should just use the camera."

So, for the remainder of the course, all fall and spring, I came to class with my camera and photographed. My photographic prints were hung and critiqued alongside the drawings and paintings of all the other students.

I had photographed for six or seven years before that class with Schorre. I was a skilled and competent photographer, but I had never thought of my photography as art until it went on the walls during Schorre's class and was critiqued by him. I remember well when he talked about the "magic" of photography, the fact that the camera "could draw every nuance of a million leaves on a tree in a thousandth of a second." I was deeply moved.

Photographs by Geoff Winningham of Charles Schorre critiquing the drawing and watercolor class in the fall of 1965.

Suddenly I saw myself as a man who was capable, literally, of performing artistic miracles. I felt, or imagined that I felt, the smoldering envy of my classmates, who struggled with pencil and paper for hours to render a human hand, then moved on to other parts of the anatomy of our model.

In one class session, where I had hung several dozen photographs on the wall for review, all made during the previous class, one of the architects asked Schorre, "Do you really think photography is art?" Those were the days before museums collected photography and before art departments offered courses in the medium, so the question was a live one at the time.

"You tell me," Schorre replied, in his instinctively Socratic way.

"Miss Evans [Elinor Evans, the much admired teacher in the architecture school at Rice in those days] says it's a folk art," one student offered.

I bristled at what I was sure had been an insult to my miraculous medium, though I actually had no idea in those days what "folk art" was. The term just sounded demeaning: not real art, just folk art. The meaning was in the inflection of the voice.

"Well, she may be right," Schorre offered. "If she is, it's a hell of a compliment, don't you think?"

The discussion ended there, and I rushed out after class to do a little research on folk art. I even found an article in a recent art periodical on the earliest daguerreotypes as folk art, and I emerged from my inquiries with a new perspective on my medium.

That discussion, Schorre's response, and my reaction to it formed only one of many critical events in my early development as a photographer. But as much as I learned and as much as I was stimulated, what I got from Schorre's class was only a fraction of what he gave me outside of class.

He invited me often to come by his studio, where he would pull out books from his substantial library. Up until that time I had no awareness at all of the great masters of photography or the body of literature that chronicled the medium's history. How could I know? The Rice library, like most every other library, had never collected photography books. But Schorre had hundreds of the classic books of the great photographers, and he loaned them to me half a dozen at a time.

Near the end of my year in his class, I applied to graduate school in photography at the Institute of Design in Chicago. With Schorre's help I produced a reasonably strong portfolio of photographs. In May, to my astonishment, I learned that I had been accepted. I declined my acceptance to law school and took off for Chicago and a life as a photographer.

It has been said that education at its best finally comes down to a teacher and a student, to the personal communication of knowledge and passion for a subject. That is the kind of education that I experienced with Charles Schorre, and that is why I treasure the memory of the man.

—Geoff Winningham

Photographs produced by Geoff Winningham during Charles Schorre's drawing and watercolor class.

Two spreads from Architecture at Rice 24, Life Class by Charles Schorre, which featured student drawings and photographs juxtaposed by Schorre's own photos and writings. The book, designed and written by Schorre, reflected his philosophies on seeing and responding to the environment around us. The American Institute of Graphic Arts included the book in the national exhibition Fifty Books of the Year.

This isn't going to be a class of instruction,
but a ground on which to discover . . . to put
the eye to work . . . to see the architecture
of things and people. I am not the teacher,
but one of the students . . . because of my
age and some experience that is not
based on architecture, I will be the . . .
monitor . . . you might say . . .
and, hopefully,
we will discover some things.
You should discover things
for yourselves and I should discover
some things for myself,
and perhaps we can share
some of these experiences.
As any creative person knows,
his own rules are the hardest. And because
you will make your own structure, or rules,
this class will probably be
both the easiest and the hardest
you have ever had.

Craft should be one's responsibility;
art, one's freedom.
For me, freedom and responsibility
cannot work without each other.
Freedom without responsibility is vegetation.
Responsibility without freedom is vacuous.
Develop your restraint and become
more self-disciplined, allowing yourself,
as a creative person, more freedom.
You must gain this yourself;
no one gives it to you . . . you have to gain it.
The gaining of freedom should allow you
to know what to do with freedom.

If you work in your uniqueness or authenticity,
using your responsibilities and freedom,
the end result or product should be authentic.
It cannot help but be authentic, for there is only
one authentic YOU. If you are at all involved,
the unique YOU should result.

If you walk out of this class at the end of the year
as a self-propelled student-teacher-student-person,
I will consider my monitoring successful.

Not everyone can draw, but I think every one of us,
no matter how crafty, can enjoy discovering—
discovering by seeing more . . .
seeing without the help of pot,
LSD, or any other crutch.
There are some things here that are naive,
perhaps childish, but you should become
more childlike if you want to get with what is
here for you. Become the you
you were before you started the first grade.

Many of us are dragging around so much
unnecessary luggage that it is almost
impossible to respond openly and uniquely
to the things that happen to us . . .
touch, sight, and sound things.
Due to visual and audial pollution,
we might even find it difficult
to avoid the fashionable,
the MOMENTous,
the ''BEEFED UP,''
and whateverthrillingexciting,
new New NEW and entertainingthing
that next comes along.

Designer, Illustrator, Photographer

By 1800, the first Classic Period waned as heroes and gods lost popularity. The Romantic Era dawned…to glorify the human spirit.

La Sylphide was a milestone in 1832…followed by decades of Romantic ballets… *Papillon*, *Giselle*. Women began to dance en pointe.

In the mid-1800's, the second great Classical Era emerged from Imperial Russia, ignited by the brilliance of Diaghilev and the *Ballets Russes*.

Houston Ballet
Ben Stevenson, *Artistic Director*

In the beginning, man was made to dance.

Charles Schorre began his career in the Houston advertising business in 1948. After a two-year stint with a small, local agency in Houston, Schorre became an art director for Foote, Cone and Belding. For four years he directed, designed, illustrated, and photographed projects for the agency's predominately oil and gas industry clients before setting out on his own as a freelancer. The skills, discipline, and thought processes involved in these early endeavors would serve him his entire career: as an artist, as a designer of his own projects, and as an illustrator for others.

Schorre always wanted to be an artist, to express himself through his own work. He took jobs as an art director and illustrator to support his family while he positioned himself to become an independent artist. But he didn't just mark time during his early career; he produced work that was regularly applauded by his peers, gathering awards locally as well as nationally.

Schorre would receive awards from the Society of Illustrators, International Typographic Society, Watercolor Society, The Art Directors Club of New York, and the American Institute of Graphic Arts. He was recognized by periodicals including *American Artist*, *Communication Arts* (graphic design), *Idea* (Japanese graphic design), and *Popular Photography*.

Opposite page: Illustrations for **Houston Ballet** *marketing brochure, 1983. Designed by Jay Loucks.*

Below: Illustration for **Hughes Tool Company**, *1959.*

"Does Fine Art automatically become Commercial Art when it is used to sell a product or service? We don't think so. It's still Fine Art — an example: Charles Schorre's painting for Hughes Tool Company. It was the top illustration prize winner in the 1959 Houston Art Guild Show."
— Communication Arts Magazine, November 1959

Left: illustrations for **Look** *magazine article by Bishop James Pike, October and November 1968. Art direction by William Hopkins.*

Left: **Seagull** *1965.*
Print, 12 x 10½ inches.
Jack and Lois Evans
Collection.

Used as a cover
illustration for
The Houston Post
Sunday Magazine,
1965.

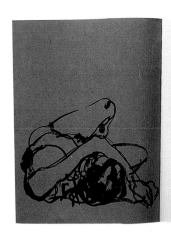

Illustrations for
The Bastard Press,
1963, a monthly
publication by the
Frank Tammen
Advertising agency,
edited by Lynn
Sweat.

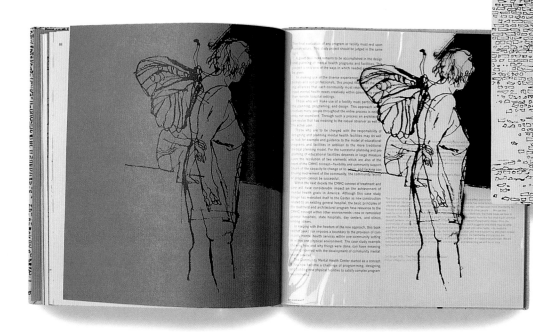

In 1963, Schorre
began traveling
throughout the
United States
observing mental
health facilities in
preparation for
coordinating the
design, illustrating,
and partially editing
a book on the plan-
ning and design for
community health
facilities.

The book **Planning,**
Programming, and
Design for The
Community Mental
Health Center, *1963.*
Art direction and
illustrations by
Charles Schorre,
design by Harrison
Allen.

Photography was a
continuing avocation
of Schorre's. At right
and on page 53 are
examples of his
work:

Nudes, *1958.*
Published in
1958 Popular
Photography
Annual.

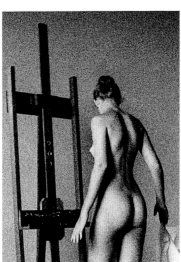

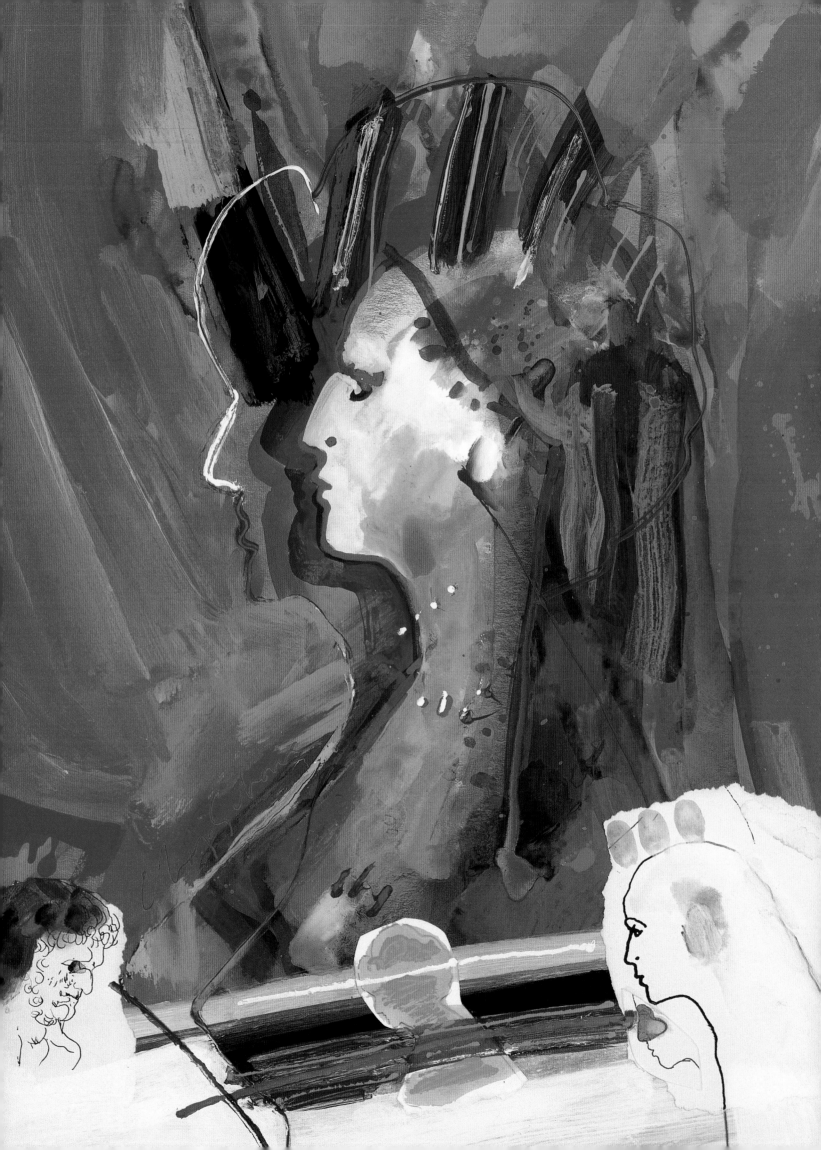

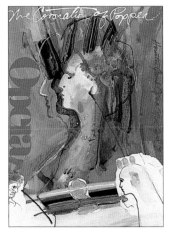

Above: **Houston Grand Opera** *poster, 1977.*

Left: **The Coronation of Poppea** *1977. Acrylic/collage on paper, 22¼ x 17 inches. David and Adair Gockley Collection.*

Right: Illustration of Marian Anderson for opening of new music auditorium, **Jones Hall,** *1966. Design by Culberson, Glass & DuBose.*

In 1968 Schorre designed, edited, and partially illustrated Life Class, *selected as one of the Fifty Best Books of the Year by the American Institute of Graphic Arts.*

Life Class, Architecture at Rice, No. 24, *1968. 78 pages, 7½ x 6 inches. Illustrations and photographs by Charles Schorre and Rice University School of Architecture students.*

Illustration for **Playboy** *magazine, November 1966. Art direction by Arthur Paul.*

Left: **Houston Grand Opera 25th Anniversary** *1980. Acrylic on canvas, 36 x 36 inches. Houston Grand Opera Collection.*

Far left: **Weegee — At Steichen's Birthday Party, MOMA, NYC** *1961. Gelatin silver print, 13½ x 10⅛ inches.*

Near left: **Edward Steichen Birthday Party, MOMA, NYC** *1961. Gelatin silver print on painted board, 13½ x 9⁹⁄₁₆ inches.*

Museum of Fine Arts, Houston, Collection.

Illustrations for **From Infancy to Infinity,** *ND. A book by William Caudill, published by Caudill Rowlett Scott and Herman Miller Inc.*

What will space for learning be like in 2000? No one knows. It will be different from what exists — that's the only certainty. Most likely by then architects and educators will have learned to raise facilities to the realm of architecture.

In the 40's and 50's the maxim was "form follows function." In the 60's and 70's it was "function follows form." The new maxim :

Form is function.

In the year 2000 sun, wind, and water may become the main sources of energy, requiring new building technology. This will affect educational facilities. There will be new ways to envelop space, new materials, new structural techniques, and new engineering to provide energy efficiency. But:

The greatest force to shape educational facilities will be education itself.

79

Artist's Handbook

WILLIAM WEGMAN
12/2/43
q. Ulsa

"I was asked by Watson-Guptill, the publisher of *American Artist* magazine, to do a 'How To' book.

"The more I got into it, the stronger I realized that I did not believe in what I was attempting to do. I did not believe in 'How To' books. . . it was never my manner of teaching.

"It was then that I also realized that if I ever did an Artist's Handbook, it would have no 'instructive words' in it. . . only photographs of the subject's face and hands.

"Since impatience and experimentation are virtues of mine, I decided to lock myself and this subject into a very simple, straightforward, but controlled situation.

"First, I ask the subject to do a certain thing: 'hold your hands up to your ears, palms facing me.' I make one or two exposures and then I ask 'Do you want to vary that in any way?' Some do and some don't — and sometimes very unexpected things happen. When you ask some people, it's almost as if you said 'Take your clothes off for a minute,' but only four people have ever refused to let me photograph them. It's usually a very intense encounter.

"Basically this series of ongoing work is a silent, visual response to the question 'How do you do it?'"

— Charles Schorre, December 5, 1988

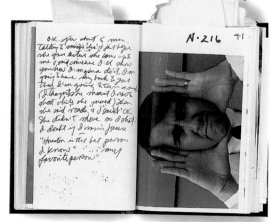

without the need for further compensation to me.

Signed

9 - 27 - 40

2 - 5 - 84

12

For a complete index of the people shown in this section, please refer to page 195.

Page 57

金子 潤

Jun Kaneko
7/13/'42

IF THESE PAGES ARE EVER PUBLISHED AS A BOOK, I WOULD
USE THE MATERIAL IN THIS MANNER:

ARTISTS
HANDBOOK

COVER

NO WORDS IN ENTIRE BOOK EXCEPT THE 2 WORDS ON

I WOULD NOT
USE A PERSON'S
NAME ESPECIALLY
IF SHE/HE IS A
SUPERSTAR.

 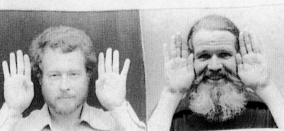  

WE ARE ALL SUPERSTARS IF WE ARE DOING IT ! RIGHT? YES!

Bob
Fowler

Don
Foster

Richard
Hunt

Betty
Fleming

Frek F.

alton Parks

I hope (wish) you have read Spread #2 because history & process of getting   to #3

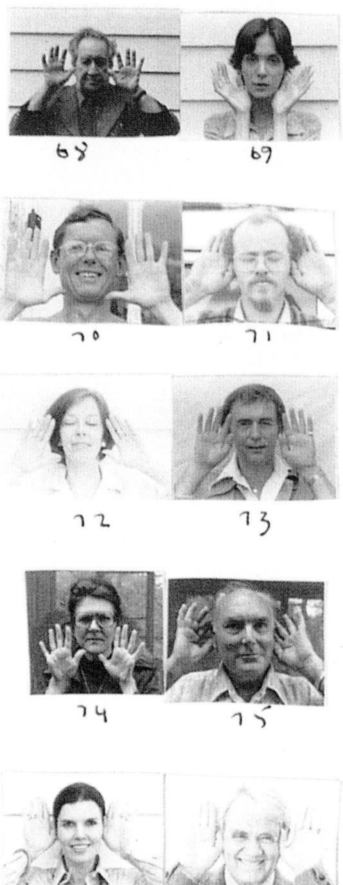

58

unnumbered pages are duplicated from "Pages #1"

60   61   68   69

62   63   70   71

64   72   73

65   66   74   75

59   67   76   77

78   79

Spread #3 from Books unpublished "Pages from Books unpublished" een very interesting 3 me as an artist/person & hopefully it is (will be) to you. Thanks. C.S.

95

80   81

I don't know what to do with this yet

82   83

84

85   86

87   88

93

89   90

91   92 (82)

94

Pages From Books Unpublished #2 1977. Photographs on illustration board, 22 x 30 inches. Museum of Fine Arts, Houston, Collection.

"Artist's Handbook" Series #2 · 27 · April · 77 © Chas Schorre

56

"Pages" from Books unpublished (Artists Handbook) Series 15.I.77

An Artist's Handbook *1977. Photographs on illustration board, 20 x 27 inches. Museum of Fine Arts, Houston, Collection.*

Saudi Arabia

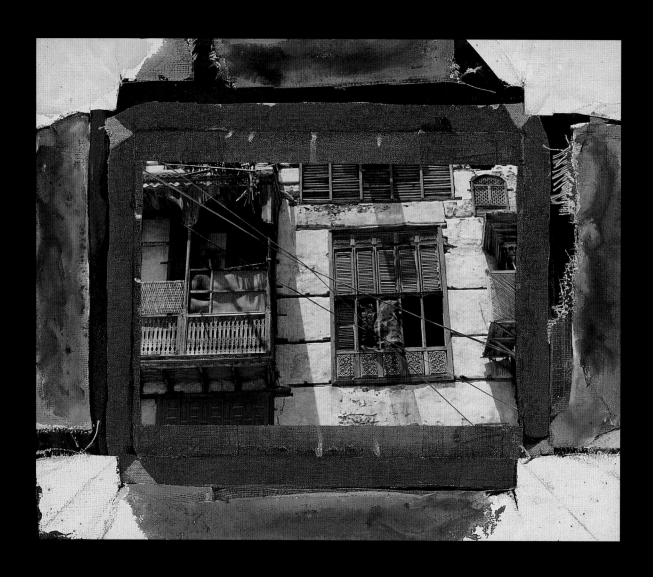

Few places or moments made more of an impression on Schorre's work than his days in Saudi Arabia, in the summer of 1979. Accepting an Artist-in-Residence grant from the Mobil Corporation, Schorre spent six weeks as a guest in Saudi Arabia, escorted around the country as he made sketches, notes, and photographs. Once back in the United States, Schorre produced a series of watercolors and collages that became part of Mobil's permanent art collection. What Mobil received for its largess was 100 works, mostly in the 16 x 20 inches size range. What Schorre received was an expanded visual vocabulary that would appear over and over again in his work: the soft, smooth shapes of the desert sand — with the accompanying palette — and the jagged shapes of the local clothing and architecture. He also acquired a changed outlook about his own ability to create:

Some of the drawing techniques Schorre used for the Mobil drawings he had used before to draw environs in West Texas or New Mexico (near left). After his trip to Saudi Arabia, however, Schorre relied more and more on photo-collage (opposite page) to incorporate his experiences into his paintings.

"But something happened to me in S. Arabia. I was sent there... an artist, 'go & react to what you see & feel.' Briefly what happened was that I could not for the first time in my life do this. I was not at liberty... to draw, paint, photograph in public... after the shock of this I became aware much more of what I was seeing. I moved into another dimension as an artist. For the first time in my life I wished for the ability of a writer who must have recall of what he witnesses. I had always reacted either at the scene or later instinctively, subconsciously.... So... for a month I was in this other dimension most of the time... from it I came to know more about freedom, awareness, meditation, observation."

Left: **Window in Jiddah, S.A.** *1979. Mixed-media collage reproduced on cover of tabloid* Photo Show #4, *size unknown. Artist's Collection.*

Above: **Signals at AR RAS Tower Entrance** *1979. Acrylic study, size unknown. Artist's Collection.*

7:30 Am

Knock on door, small child stuck out his hand to shake and ask quite questions which I could naturally not understand. Told him to wait until I awakened A - then he was gone. Five minutes later his smaller brother appeared nicely "thobed" carrying pot hot metal covered pitcher of ~~hot~~ sweetened fresh milk.

— There are two women in alphalpha field now working about 75 yds away now they are putting their black Thobes on because they see me. Before they had them around ~~heads, but not should~~ heads, but not faces.

— "What do you think about our country?" "Oh, everything has been wonderful. I like the people, the landscape. It will be interesting to see how things develop in the next 5-10 years." I believe, after having been here a few weeks, that the best way for me to understand what's going on is to erase what & how I think as much as possible and observe as deeply and as quietly as one can & just let it be ... because there is really no way I can describe except on surface. There is so much money among all this (seemingly to me) poverty etc. First you might think some are lazy, but then you see some very industrious ones just like any other country. You have to re-adjust your value system. Hold back. Listen. A. told me very authoritatively "This is where they keep all the animals." Next moment B. told me "this is where we all gather as a family & have fun."

Abdallah is only 24, but this drawing came out as
he might be 10 yrs. from now. J Souza "Dallah".

"Working from within:
only early in my life
did I ever go out, sit
down, or stand up and
paint on location. I
feel more comfortable,
can see in depth. . .
even meditate into
things seen by using a
camera and/or quick
sketchbook. . . quick,
like sketching from
an automobile going
40–60 mph (this came
to me while working
in Saudi Arabia in
1979). . . essence,
residue. . . this is what
I end up with and this
for me is the best way
to obtain it."

RED . 1 ?

watchtower in distance superimposed on
fortress ruins in foreground ½'cl R—
Saudi Arab
May. 79
Nov. 5 Mon

56

needs glasses on
Too timid

old woman at
airport whose feet
fit in slippers the
way

...and bad laundry day.

6

11

*Sketches and notes
from the sketchbook
diaries made while
in Saudi Arabia.
Center, the small
photo albums made
from Schorre's prints
once back in the
United States.*

I was asked not to photograph women in S. Arabia. It was only after I processed film did I realize 2 women were in this foreground.

Left: **Untitled** *1979. Photograph. Artist's Collection.*

Below: **Saudi Arabia '79** *1979. Watercolor on paper, 19½ x 25½ inches. Artist's Collection.*

This is not a good drawing but best I can do
from imagination. I had just finished
a neat drawing about an hour ago of this bread
bike. He was stopped at a busy corner so I
went off in an alley by a fabric store where I figured
no one would notice. Just as I finished I found
the store man at my side looking at the drawing.
He was very angry in attempting to tear the drawing
out of this book so I ablieged him & did it
for him hoping he would feel better. Instead
he tore it up into little pieces & dropped it in
front of me. I left before he called police.

There are several pages out of this
book & this has been what's happened to
them. I'm lucky they didn't take the book,
read it or jail me.

Left: **Untitled** *1979. Mixed-media collage on canvas with torn canvas, size unknown. Artist's Collection.*

Above: **Red Sea Sunset • Jiddah Harbor** *1979. Print, 30 x 20 inches. Mobil Corporation Collection.*

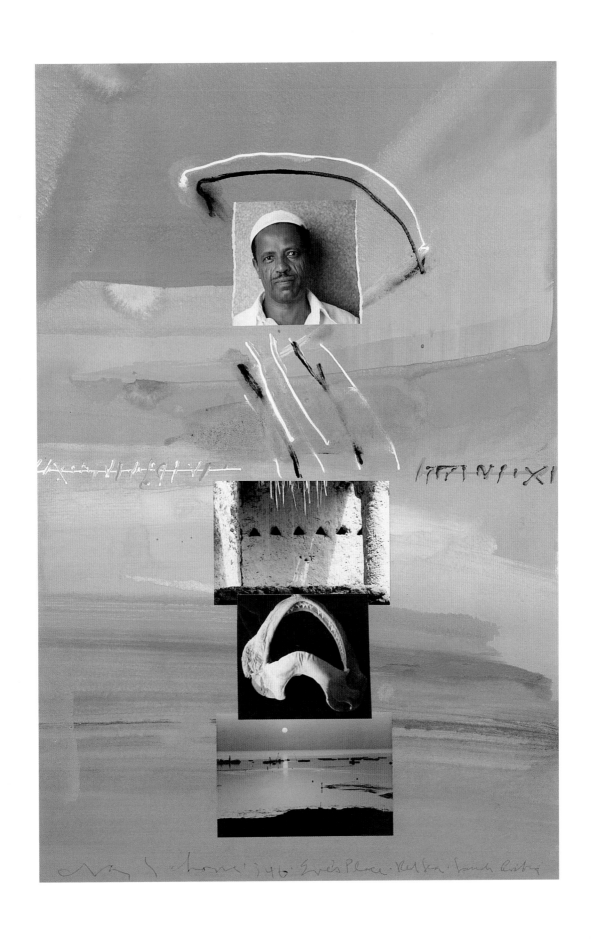

Left: Photographs from scrapbooks and inset of watercolor study, 1979. Artist's Collection.

Above: **Eve's Place • Red Sea • Saudi Arabia (#346)** *ND. Mixed-media collage on paper, 23 x 15 inches. Artist's Collection.*

Page 77

Left: **I Cross My Heart and Hope To. . .** *ND. Acrylic, "gold" spray paint on paper, approx. 8 x 8 inches. Artist's Collection.*

Above: **Near Yanbu, Saudi Arabia** *ND. Photo collage on paper, 22½ x 14¼ inches. Frederic and Betty Fleming Collection.*

Pages From Books

Unpublished

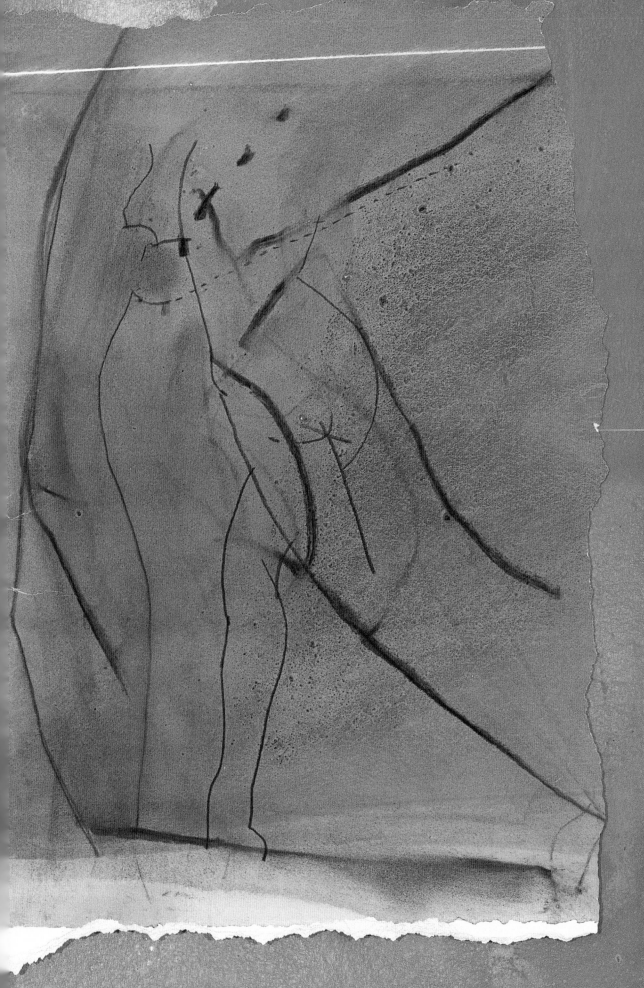

Pages From Books Unpublished #284 *N.D. Mixed-media collage, 22¼ x 30 inches. Jim Tiebout Collection.*

"Pages... from Books unpublished" is an extended series that has been on-going for more than 17 yrs... ... and characterizes my work as a whole... in that I use drawings, photographs and paintings as informants to each other. I use only my own work for collaging as opposed to using found print matter etc. of others. This I do for many reasons, but most of all because it is more personal

and difficult. The collages are residue or evidence of my seeing... using a particular instrument (camera) coupled with hand marking that are juxtaposed. ... sometimes deliberately - sometimes accidentally, according to what has gone on or going on in my mind head at the time.

The studios where I work daily are similar to an archiological dig - scattered drawings, photographs, painting and their combinations

on the walls, floors and tables... all are very different but, of equal importance to me - like our children and grandchildren (8) one moves, provokes a move from the other... I move, the work moves + in turn causes me to again move etc.

I hope the pieces are about polarities, seeing, similarities mystery, provocation, sometimes terror, beauty, grace, joy

wit, re-seeing the common, + seeing the ordinary in another way.

During the process I try + keep the work in doubt as long as possible. If I find the path too clear me or less going, I stop and go in another direction. I'm not doing this for boredom, money or fame... although you can't help receiving some of each along the way.

31.1.0[?]

Joe Sch[?]

"Pages. . . from Books Unpublished" is an extended series that has been on-going for more than 17 yrs. . . . . .and characterizes my work as a whole. . . in that I use drawings, photo-graphs and paintings as informants to each other.

—

I use only my own work for collaging as opposed to using found print matter etc. of others. This I do for many reasons, but most of all because it is more personal and difficult. The collages are residue of evidence of my seeing. . . using a parti-cular instrument (camera) coupled with hand marking that are juxta-posed. . . sometimes accidentally, accord-ing to what has gone on or going on in my ~~mind~~ head at the time.

The studios where I work daily are similar to an archio-logical dig. Scattered drawings, photographs, paintings and their combinations on the walls, floors and tables. . . all are very different but, of equal importance to me — like our children and grand-children (8) one move pro-vokes a move from the other. . . I move, the work moves & in turn causes me to again move etc.

—

I hope the pieces are about polarities, see-ing, similarities, mystery, magic, provocation, sometimes terror, beauty, grace, joy wit, re-see-ing the common & seeing the ordinary in another way.

During the ✳ process I try & keep the work in doubt as long as possible. If I find the path too clear to me or easy going, I stop and go in an-other direction. I'm not doing this for bore-dom, money or fame. . . although you can't help re-ceiving some of each along the way.

31 • 1 • 90

Chas. Schorre

25·AP·77·

I'VE SPENT MOST OF MY LIFETIME (BORN 9 MAR 25) DRAWING AND PAINTING,...
WHAT SOME PEOPLE CALL "FINE ART" DRAWING AND PAINTING. FOR MANY YEARS
WE SUPPORTED THIS HABIT AND OUR FAMILY BY DRAWING AND PAINTING THINGS
FOR "FAST MONEY"... NOW I MAKE MARKS & THINGS AS I'M COMPELLED OR
WHEN I DESIRE AND IF SOMEONE SEES IT, LIKES IT ENOUGH TO PAY
FOR IT, WE GET THE MONEY IF & WHEN THEY DESIRE.

LOOKING BACK AT THE WORK DONE & WHAT I'M DOING NOW, I KINDA LIKE
THE VARIETY OF EXPERIENCE, THE DIFFERENT TYPES OF PEOPLE I'VE
WORKED WITH ... AND TO ME, IT HAS ALL BEEN "FINE ART" BE-
CAUSE IT WAS THE FINEST I COULD DO AT THE TIME & I WAS
USUALLY WHISTLING OR PLAYING JAZZ TAPES WHILE DOING IT
SO IT MUST HAVE ALSO BEEN JOYOUS MOST OF THAT TIME.

VARIETY OF EXPERIENCE: I MUST LIKE THAT BECAUSE I'M STILL WORK-
ING IN MANY DIRECTIONS ... DIRECTIONS THAT ARE DICTATED BY MOODS &
MATERIAL.

WHAT HAS BECOME AN UNEXPECTED THRILL IS THE RELATEDNESS, THE CONNECTION
OF ALL THESE DIRECTIONS. THEY SEEM TO BE ALL OF THE SAME VISUAL
AND SPIRITUAL SOURCE WHEN ~~VIEWED~~ REVIEWED FROM A DISTANCE
LIKE SEEING RELATED DESIGN FROM 30,000 FT.

[LOOKING BACK EVERY NOW & THEN WHILE WORKING FORWARD PUTS
ME IN THE SOLID TENSION OF NOW.]
WHAT I WAS ISN'T NOW WAS IT?!

NOW

MIGGIE SCHORRE (CHIMAYO·N·MEX·76)

NATURAL PEOPLE ARE YOUTH FULL

"ART AIN'T NOTHING...IT'S KEEPING BUSY
THAT COUNTS" GRANDMA MOSES VIA PA
CAPONIGRO. OKAY, MAYBE, BUT LOOK
AROUND WHILE DREAMING AND NOT THINKIN
OR EVEN NOT LOOKING AND YOU WILL USUAL
SEE SOMETHING.

IS IT?
REALLY AND TRUELY?
TRUE REALLY?
IS IT?
IS IT?
IT IS?
REALLY NOW,
REALLY REAL...
REALLY IT ISN'T
IS IT REALLY?
TRUELY ISN'T
WHAT IS REAL
REALLY IS IT?
WHAT IS IT REALLY AND TRUELY?
IS THE "REAL" REALLY?
REALLY AND TRUELY
AND DO IT! HUNDREDS OF TIMES!

IS IT?
IT ISN'T.
IT ISN'T!
IT IS

"PAGES FROM BOOKS UNPUBLISHED" STARTED WITH ME ~~ABOUT~~ 5 YRS. AGO. ... NO, I
GUESS IT STARTED BEFORE THAT. ABOUT 7 YRS. AGO I STARTED A "HANDBOOK",
HANDS OF PEOPLE WHO STILL USED THEIR HANDS FOR "MAKING THEIR LIVING"
TRIED TO GET A GRANT, NO GRANT, FORGOT ABOUT IT FOR A YEAR OR SO
HANDS OF FRIENDS, CRAFTSMEN-WOMEN, ARTISTS, ~~THESE~~

THEN IT VERY NATURALLY EVOLVED INTO SERIES OF ARTIST
HEAD·HAND STRAIGHT PHOTOGRAPHS. (~~WE~~ WHEN I WRITE/SAY
"ARTIST", I ALSO MEAN "PHOTOGRAPHER", BUT WHEN I WRITE
"PHOTOGRAPHER" I DO NOT ALWAYS MEAN "ARTIST".

PAINTINGS OF THE NUDE FEMALE. NO WORDS EXCEPT THESE AFTERWORDS, "GET ANY GOOD, WORKABLE, DRAWING, PAINTING, PHOTO VIA TOTAL INSTRUMENT

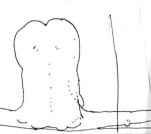

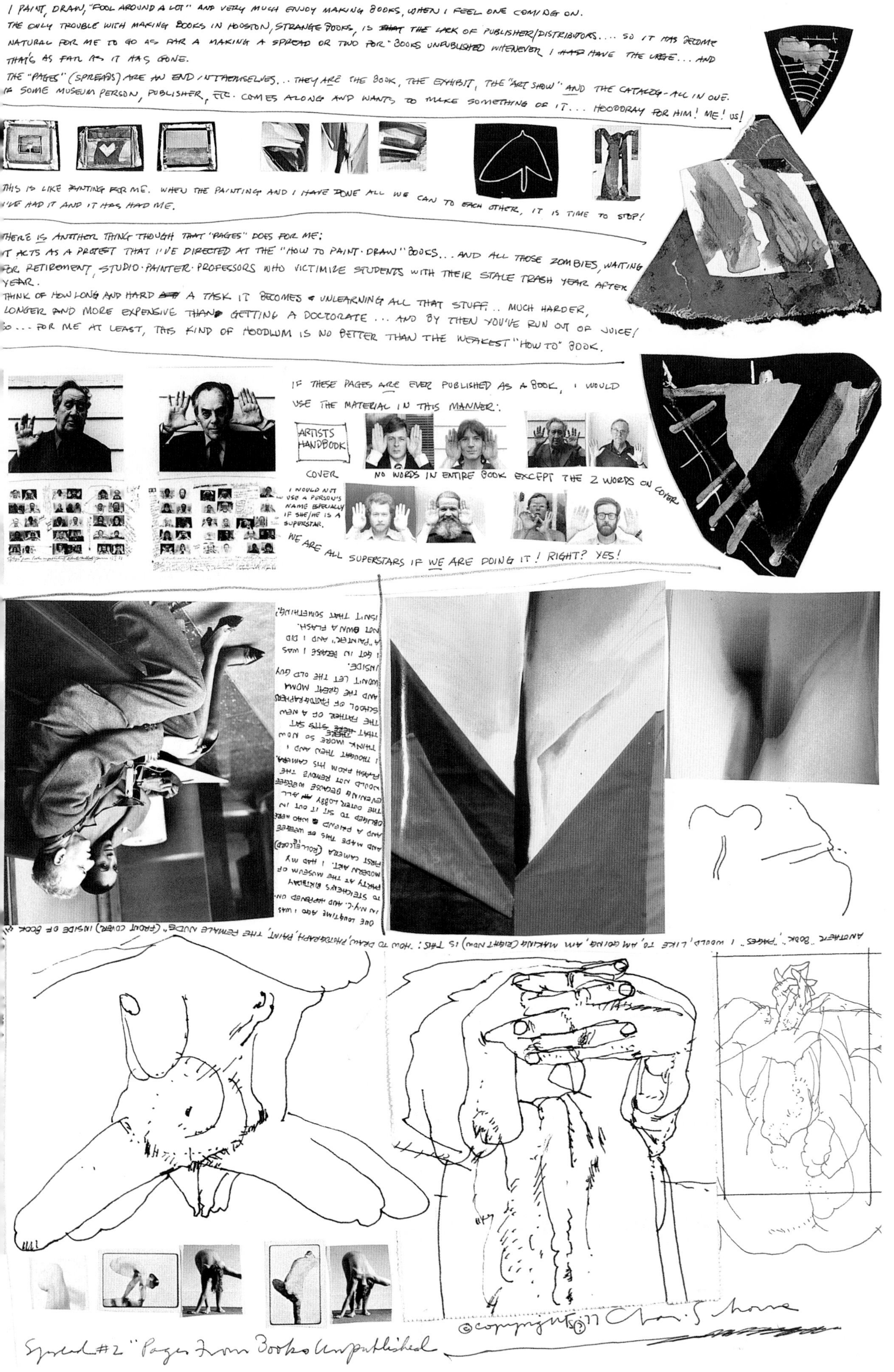

I PAINT, DRAW, "FOOL AROUND A LOT" AND VERY MUCH ENJOY MAKING BOOKS, WHEN I FEEL ONE COMING ON.

THE ONLY TROUBLE WITH MAKING BOOKS IN HOUSTON, STRANGE BOOKS, IS THAT THE LACK OF PUBLISHER/DISTRIBUTORS.... SO IT HAS BECOME NATURAL FOR ME TO GO AS FAR A MAKING A SPREAD OR TWO FOR "BOOKS UNPUBLISHED WHENEVER I HAD HAVE THE URGE... AND THAT'S AS FAR AS IT HAS GONE.

THE "PAGES" (SPREADS) ARE AN END IN THEMSELVES... THEY ARE THE BOOK, THE EXHIBIT, THE "ART SHOW" AND THE CATALOG-ALL IN ONE. IF SOME MUSEUM PERSON, PUBLISHER, ETC. COMES ALONG AND WANTS TO MAKE SOMETHING OF IT... HOOORAY FOR HIM! ME! US!

THIS IS LIKE PAINTING FOR ME. WHEN THE PAINTING AND I HAVE DONE ALL WE CAN TO EACH OTHER, IT IS TIME TO STOP! I'VE HAD IT AND IT HAS HAD ME.

THERE IS ANOTHER THING THOUGH THAT "PAGES" DOES FOR ME:

IT ACTS AS A PROTEST THAT I'VE DIRECTED AT THE "HOW TO PAINT·DRAW" BOOKS... AND ALL THOSE ZOMBIES, WAITING FOR RETIREMENT, STUDIO·PAINTER·PROFESSORS WHO VICTIMIZE STUDENTS WITH THEIR STALE TRASH YEAR AFTER YEAR.

THINK OF HOW LONG AND HARD A TASK IT BECOMES & UNLEARNING ALL THAT STUFF... MUCH HARDER, LONGER AND MORE EXPENSIVE THAN GETTING A DOCTORATE ... AND BY THEN YOU'VE RUN OUT OF JUICE!

SO... FOR ME AT LEAST, THIS KIND OF HOODLUM IS NO BETTER THAN THE WEAKEST "HOW TO" BOOK.

IF THESE PAGES ARE EVER PUBLISHED AS A BOOK, I WOULD USE THE MATERIAL IN THIS MANNER:

ARTISTS HANDBOOK

COVER

NO WORDS IN ENTIRE BOOK EXCEPT THE 2 WORDS ON COVER

I WOULD NOT USE A PERSON'S NAME ESPECIALLY IF SHE/HE IS A SUPERSTAR.

WE ARE ALL SUPERSTARS IF WE ARE DOING IT! RIGHT? YES!

ONE LONG TIME AGO I WAS IN N.Y.C. AND HURRIED ON TO STEICHEN'S BIRTHDAY PARTY AT THE MUSEUM OF MODERN ART. I HAD MY FIRST CAMERA (ROLLEIFLEX) AND MADE THIS OR WHERE AND A FRIEND & WHO WERE OBLIGED TO SIT IT OUT IN THE OUTER LOBBY ALL EVENING BECAUSE I COULD NOT REMOVE THE FLASH FROM HIS CAMERA. I THOUGHT THEN AND I THINK MORE SO NOW THAT THESE SITS SAT THE FATHER OF A NEW SCHOOL OF PHOTOGRAPHERS AND THE GREAT MOMA WOULDN'T LET THE OLD GUY INSIDE. I GOT IN BECAUSE I WAS A "PAINTER", AND I DID NOT OWN A FLASH. ISN'T THAT SOMETHING?

ANOTHER BOOK "PAGES". I WOULD, LIKE TO, AM GOING, AM MAKING (RIGHT NOW) IS THIS: "HOW TO DRAW, PHOTOGRAPH, PAINT, THE FEMALE NUDE". (FRONT COVER), INSIDE OF BOOK R.

Spread #2 "Pages From Books Unpublished

©copyright '77

Pages From Books Unpublished #38 *ND. Mixed-media collage, 15 x 23 inches. Jim Tiebout Collection.*

Pages From Books Unpublished #161 *1981. Mixed-media collage, 20 x 26 inches. Museum of Fine Arts, Houston, Collection.*

C.S. ·20·VII·80

Pages From Books Unpublished #147 *1989. Mixed-media collage, 15½ x 22 inches. Artist's Collection.*

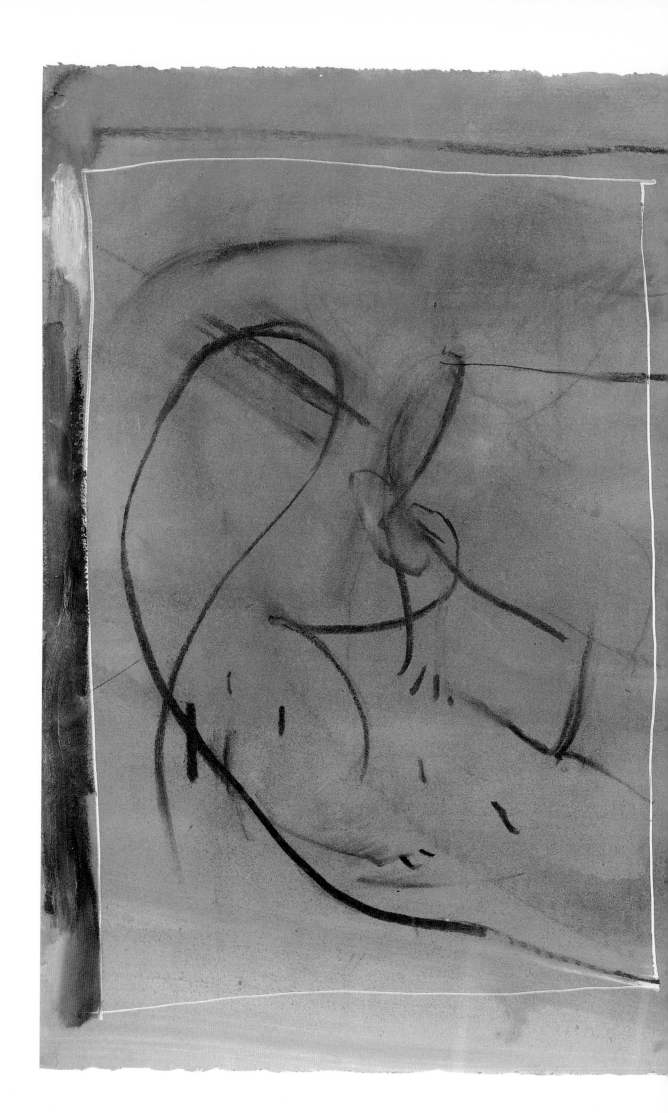

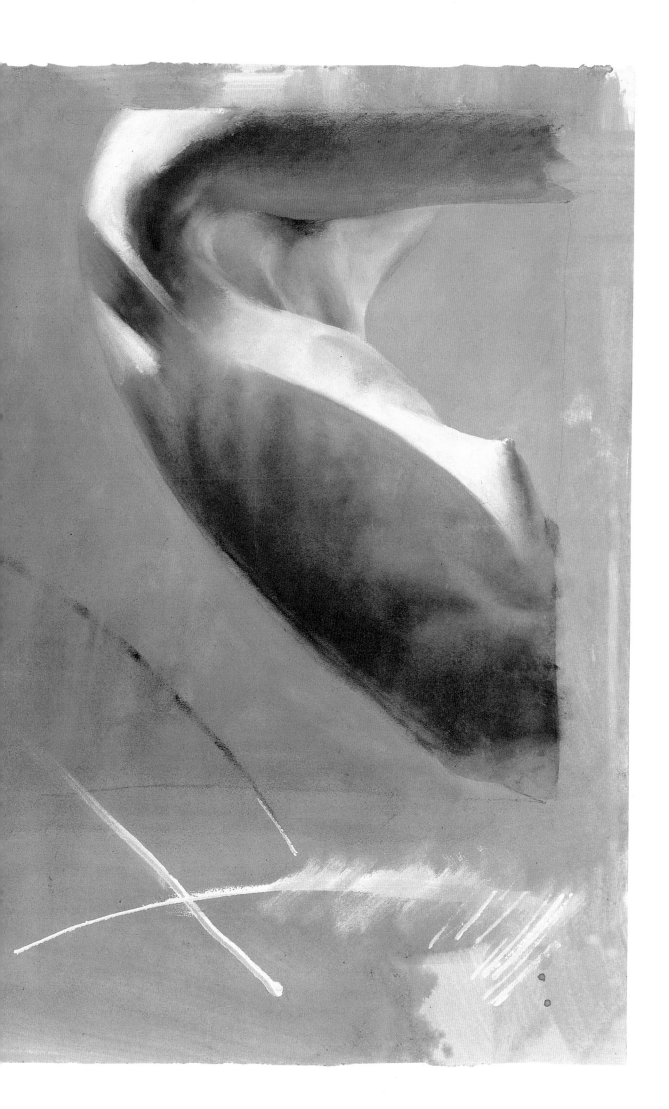

Pages From Books Unpublished #169 *1981. Mixed-media collage, 22 x 30 inches. Artist's Collection.*

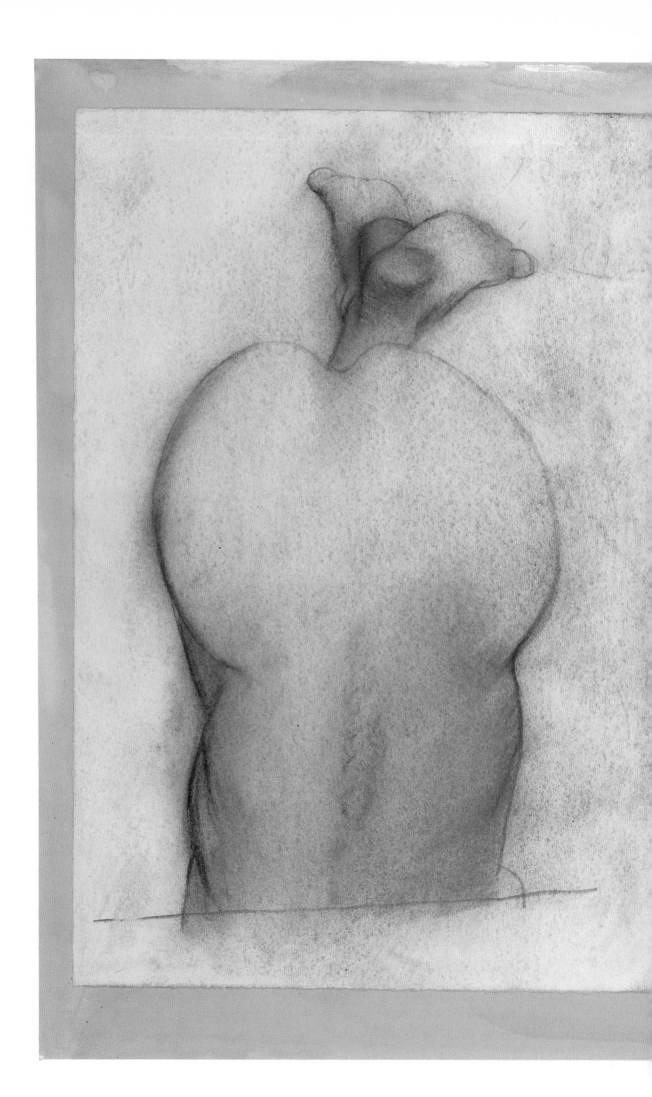

1 2 3 4 5 6 7 8 9 10 10 12 13 14

27

Pages From Books Unpublished #174 *1981. Mixed-media collage, 23 x 30 inches. Artist's Collection.*

Pages From Books Unpublished #291 *1984. Mixed-media collage, 22 x 30 inches. Artist's Collection.*

Pages From Books Unpublished (Untitled) *ND. Mixed-media collage, 22 x 30 inches. Artist's Collection.*

194 Chas. Stone

Pages From Books Unpublished #498 *ND. Mixed-media collage, 22 x 30 inches. Artist's Collection.*

Sketchbook

Much of Schorre's work will
never be seen. It will lie in the
dark, sandwiched between layers
of paper, filed away on shelves.
The work will remain in his
vast number of sketchbooks:
series after series of drawings,
watercolors, cut and paste
collages, and notations tucked
quietly away out of sight.
Certainly not all the sketches
are worth seeing, for they were
surely loose investigations. But
the vitality and pure joy of
expression that comes from these
pages are pleasant to experience.
The pages from the sketchbook
shown here are life studies, some
drawn directly into the booklet,
some cut out and attached.
Although not all of Schorre's
sketches are signed, the drawings
in this booklet are, and all seem
to have been signed at the same
time.

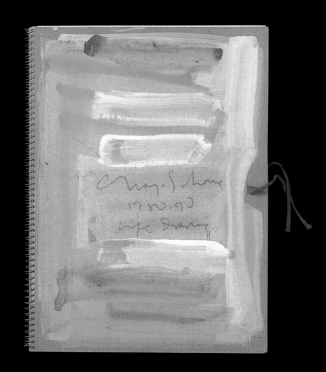

Chas. Schorre 1980 · 90 Life Drawing
*1980-90. Drawings, watercolor,
and collage in a 13 x 10-inch
booklet of 57 numbered pages.
Artist's Collection.*

57

34 #6 NEW -16

Pages 11, 18-19, 25; 45,

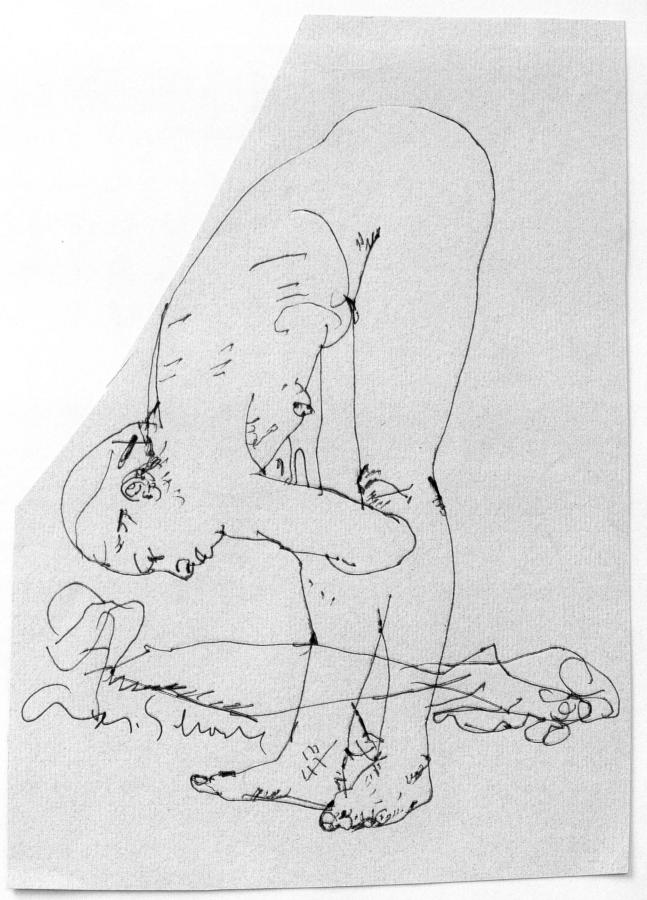

35

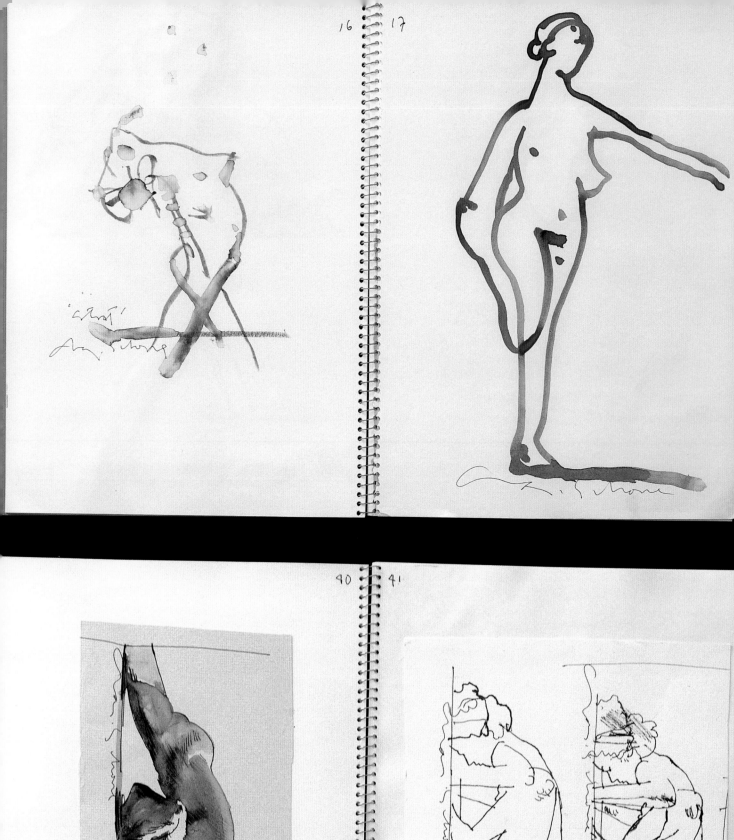

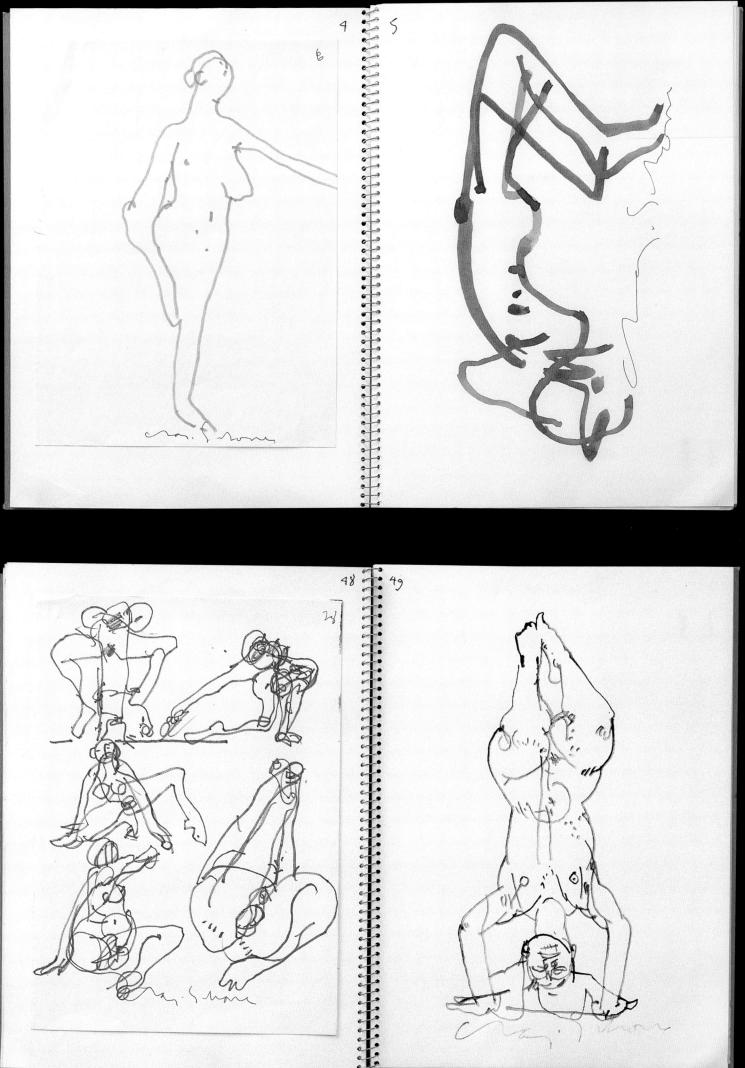

Selected Works

336 Narrative Follows Purchase *ND. Mixed-media collage on paper, 22½ x 30 inches. Artist's Collection.*

"No one or group knows it yet, but the way to work is by working…and looking very little, if not at all, over your shoulder at what might be going on around you.…"

Left: **Colored Crosses** *1977. Mixed-media collage, 22 x 30 inches. Martha and Will Botts Collection.*

Above: **Camelwalk I** *1982. Acrylic on canvas, 48 x 48 inches. Jacksonville Hilton Collection.*

Triptych *1992. Acrylic on canvas, three 6 x 4-foot panels. Jerry and Sandy Herring Collection.*

Page 117

Above: **Connected Celebration** *1973. Acrylic on canvas, 84 x 84 inches. Frederic and Betty Fleming Collection.*

Right: **Texas Primrose** *1982. Graphite rub with original plate, 20 x 30 inches. Rick and Mary Gardner Collection.*

Left: **Nude standing on one leg** *1975. Acrylic on paper, 30 x 22 inches. Artist's Collection.*

Right: **Tripod** *1977. Acrylic on paper, 30 x 22 inches. Artist's Collection.*

Page 120

Left: **Bentotem** *ND. Acrylic on paper, 30 x 22 inches. Artist's Collection.*

Right: **Nude Headstand** *ND. Acrylic on paper, 30 x 22 inches. Artist's Collection.*

Page 121

King's X *1992. Oil on canvas, 48 x 48 inches. Artist's Collection.*

"I'm teaching myself art and trying to leave as much evidence as possible around as artifacts — soulcraft — something more than just a tombstone. But I'm also trying to have as much joy as possible while I'm doing it."

Eakin'spirit *ND. Mixed-media collage on paper, 22 x 30 inches. Artist's Collection.*

Untitled *1977. Acrylic on canvas, 57 x 65 inches. Frederic and Betty Fleming Collection.*

Crossignal *1983. Acrylic on canvas, 36 x 36 inches. Lomis Slaughter Collection.*

Tamarind • Little Egypt (Starmakers) *1979-80. Acrylic on paper, 26 x 26 inches. Artist's Collection.*

Untitled *ND. Acrylic on canvas with torn canvas, 23½ x 23½ inches. Artist's Collection.*

"I know one thing 'for sure'... I'm shedding some skin and getting it lean and simple...."

Untitled *1993. Mixed-media collage on paper, 22½ x 30 inches. Jerry and Sandy Herring Collection.*

Maestro *1983. Acrylic on canvas, 36 x 36 inches. Lomis Slaughter Collection.*

Page 129

Angeltrap *ND. Mixed-media collage on canvas, 60 x 60 inches. Artist's Collection.*

Untitled *1992. Acrylic on paper, 22 x 30 inches. Artist's Collection.*

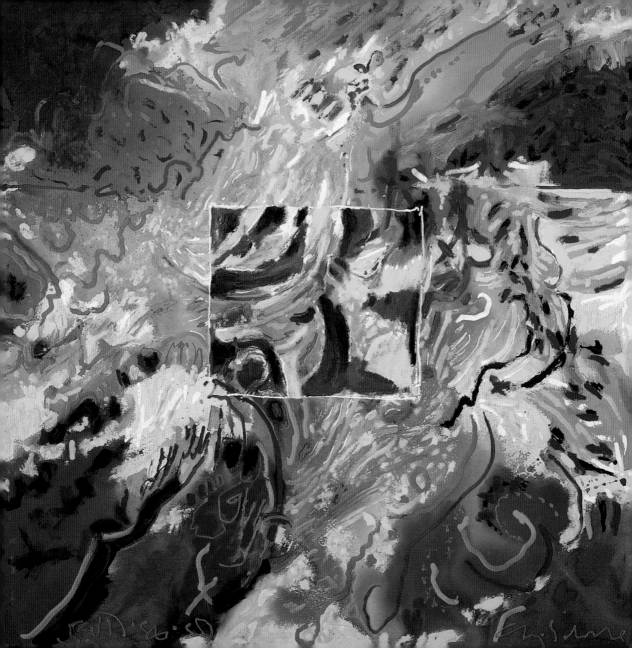

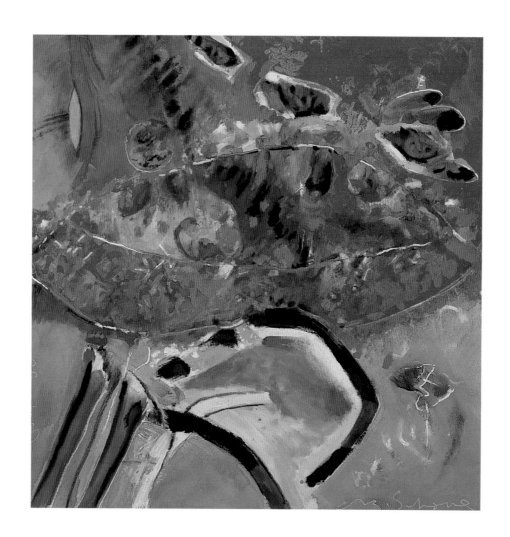

*"If you have a beautiful
method, but nothing to
reveal. . . no magic. . .
you literally have nothing."*

Left: **Earthstargarden** *1986. Acrylic on canvas, 48 x 48 inches. Artist's Collection.*

Above: **Greed Sucking Stars from the Heavens** *1987. Acrylic on canvas, 48 x 48 inches. Artist's Collection.*

Page 133

Above: **Starace** *ND. Acrylic on canvas, 27 x 49 inches. Artist's Collection.*

Below: **Powerplace** *1991. Acrylic on canvas, 48 x 48 inches. Artist's Collection.*

Starmaker *1988. Acrylic on canvas, 36 x 48 inches. Artist's Collection.*

*"One thing leads to another…
it all adds up…there is a
pattern…this is life."*

When Loveliness Met Terror *ND. Acrylic on canvas, 16 x 30 inches. Artist's Collection.*

Moonbloom *ND. Acrylic on canvas, 48 x 48 inches. Artist's Collection.*

Cardinalanguage
ND. Acrylic on canvas, 36 x 48 inches. Artist's Collection.

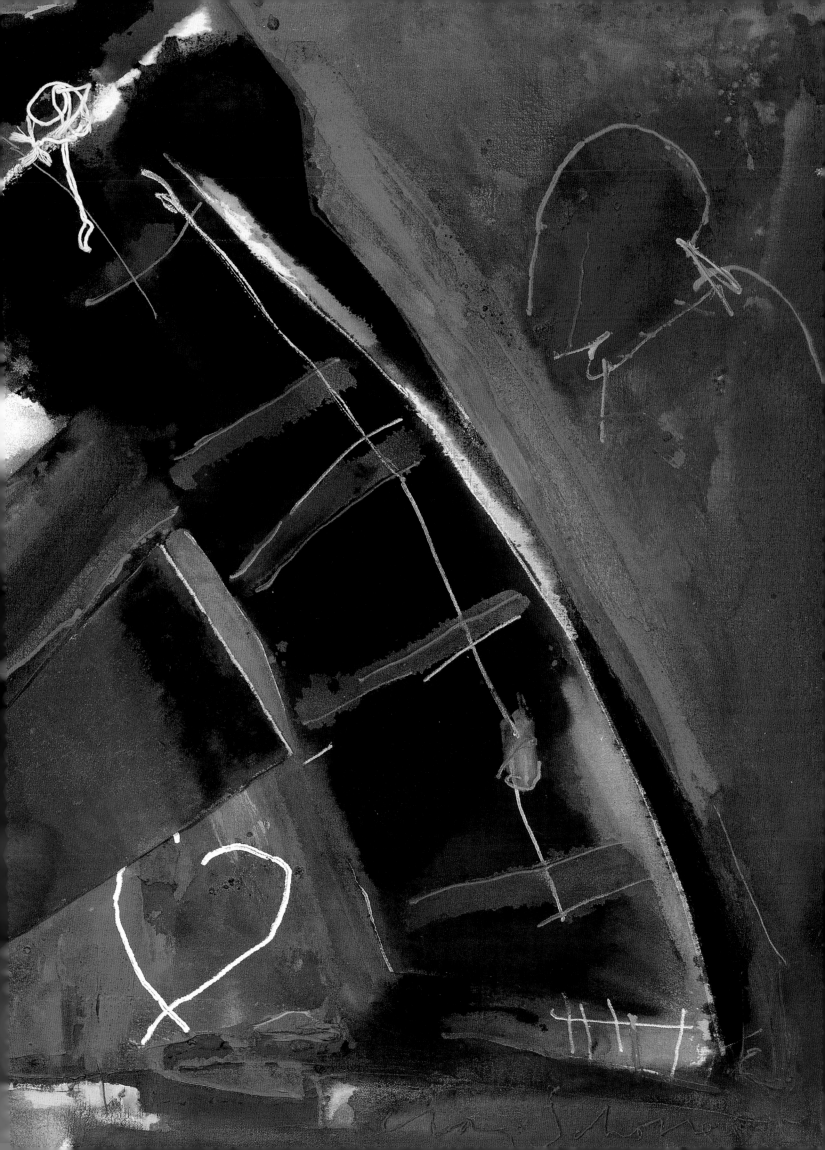

Left: **Bonescream** *1985. Acrylic and charcoal on canvas, 36 x 36 inches. Jacksonville Hilton Collection.*

Above: **Blue Mosque, Saudi Arabia — Trampas, New Mexico** *ND. Photographs, 9¾ x 13 inches. Priscilla Blohm Collection.*

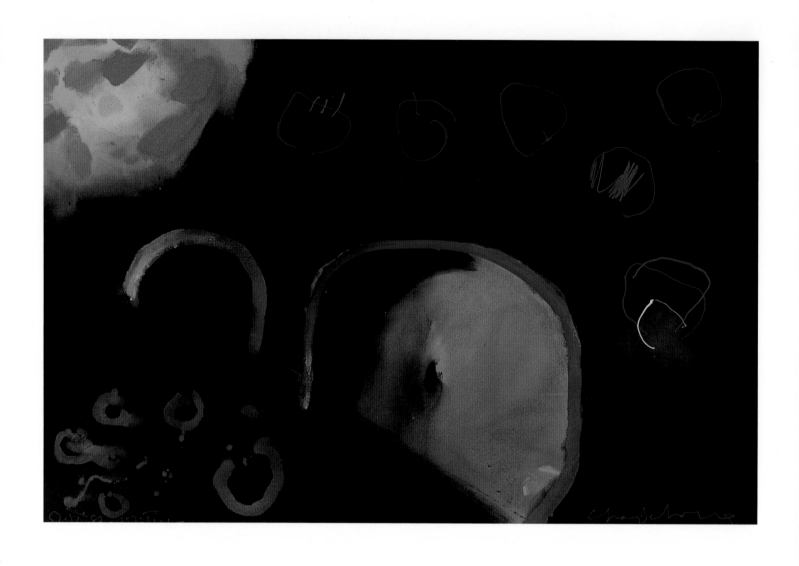

Above: **Moonavel** *1984. Acrylic on canvas, dimensions unknown. Museum of Fine Arts, Houston, Collection.*

Right: **Shellmoon 381** *ND. Mixed-media collage on paper, 30 x 22½ inches. William and Jeanette Pakalka Collection.*

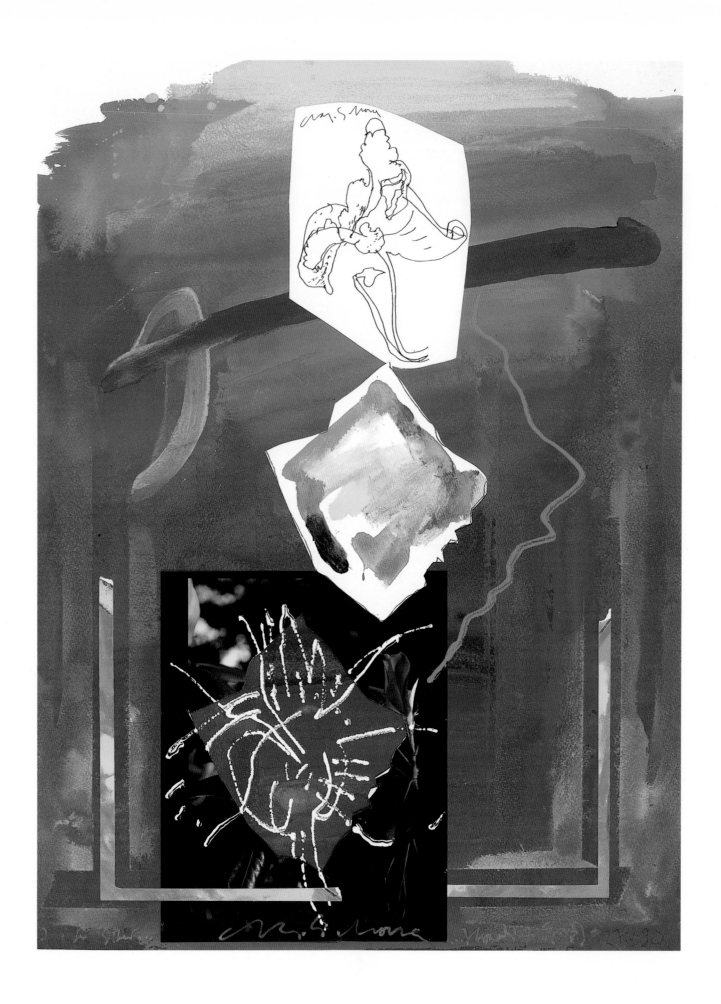

Twi-Lite Show *1987/1990. Mixed-media collage on paper, 24 x 18 inches. Artist's Collection.*

Untitled *1980. Acrylic on paper, 24 x 18 inches. Artist's Collection.*

Series of three:

Dark Entrances *1987.*
Lithograph,
17³⁄₁₆ x 20⁵⁄₁₆ inches.

Secret Universe *1987.*
Lithograph,
17¼ x 22³⁄₈ inches.

Ancient Memories *1987.*
Lithograph,
17³⁄₈ x 22⁷⁄₁₆ inches.

Museum of Fine Arts,
Houston, Collection.

Page 146

Untitled *ND. Charcoal on paper, 25¾ x 19½ inches. Bob and Andrea Lapsley Collection.*

Page 147

Firstsign *1976. Mixed-media collage, 25½ x 21½ inches. Artist's Collection.*

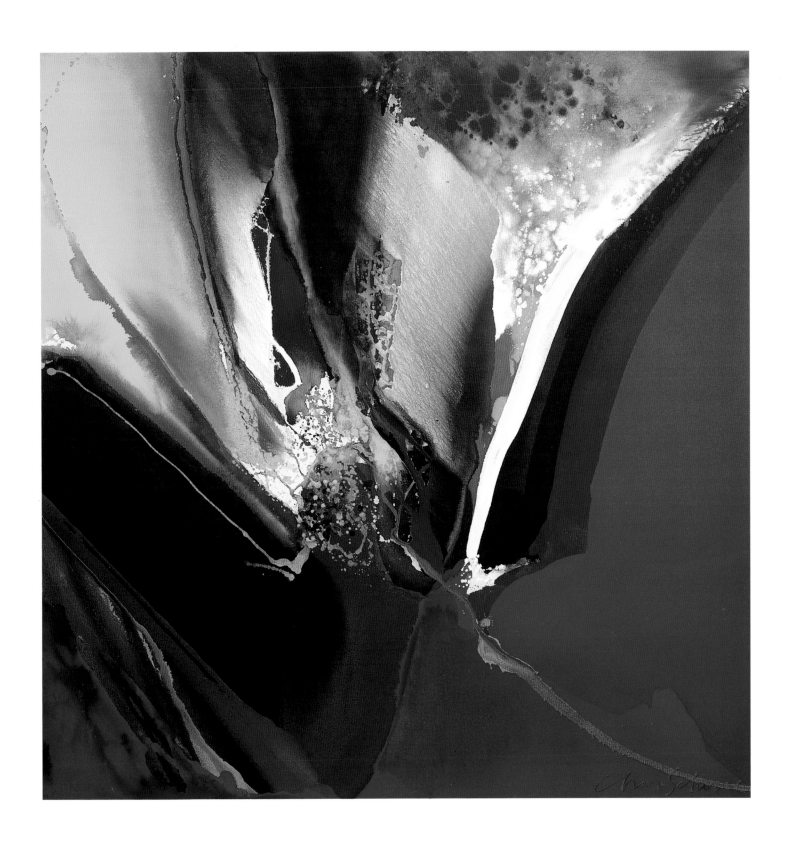

Earthburst *ND. Acrylic on canvas, 60 x 60 inches. Jess Kaps Collection.*

Mary's Tomato *1988. Watercolor and acrylic on paper, 23 x 16 inches. Mary Gardner Collection.*

Lightouch *1981. Acrylic on canvas, 60 x 60 inches. Janita Lo Collection.*

Page 151

Untitled *1990. Mixed-media collage on paper, 22¼ x 29 inches. Artist's Collection.*

Untitled *ND. Acrylic on paper, 22¼ x 30½ inches. Artist's Collection.*

"Good characteristics for painting for me are: in doubt, outrageousness, mysteriously beautiful, unidentifiable elegance, always inventive and uniquely my own."

Left: **Springsign** ND. *Acrylic on canvas, 48 x 36½ inches. Hines Collection.*

Above: **Earthbirth II** ND. *Acrylic on canvas, 66 x 66 inches. Hines Collection.*

Page 155

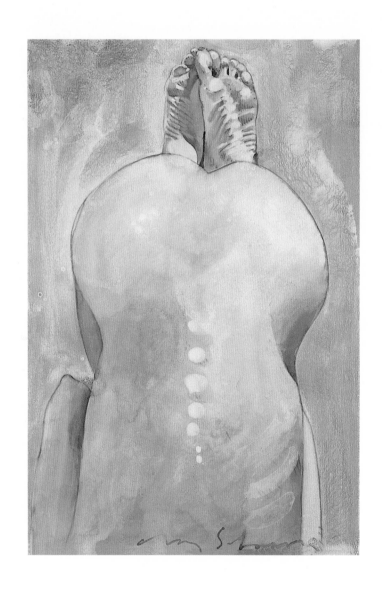

Above: **Untitled** ND. *Acrylic on paper, 18 x 12¼ inches. Maurice Lewis Collection.*

Right: **Untitled** 1990. *Mixed-media collage on paper, 24 x 18 inches. Artist's Collection.*

10·i·90

Sandstar Moondancing *1986. Oil on canvas, 36 x 48 inches. Artist's Collection.*

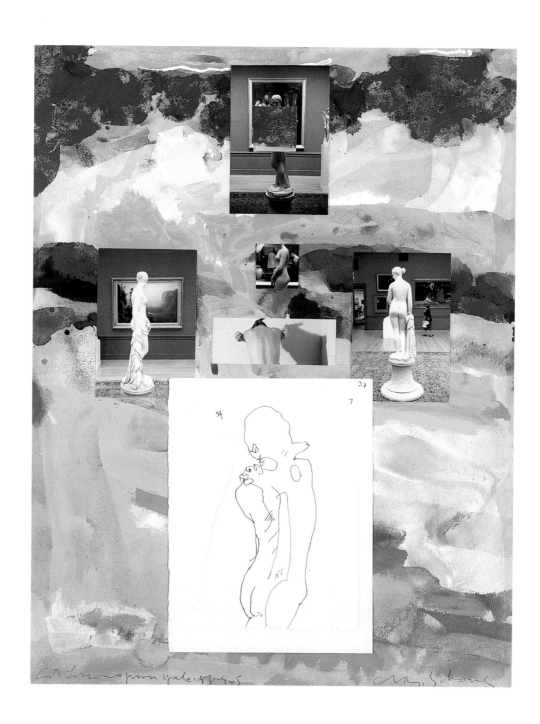

Art Lessons from Yale *1988. Mixed-media collage on canvas, 25½ x 19¼ inches. Artist's Collection.*

Untitled *1982. Acrylic on paper, 30 x 23 inches. Barth and Jane Schorre Collection.*

Untitled *1990. Acrylic on paper, 30 x 23¾ inches. Barth and Jane Schorre Collection.*

Page 161

Above: **Untitled** *1983. Acrylic on canvas, 78 x 224 inches. Interfin Corporation Collection.*

Below: **Untitled** *1983. Acrylic on canvas, 78 x 224 inches. Interfin Corporation Collection.*

Signal for 2nd Chance *ND. Mixed-media collage on paper, 22¾ x 29¾ inches. Angela and Cyril Arney Collection.*

Left, above: **Untitled** *1981. Acrylic on canvas, 48 x 48 inches. Interfin Corporation Collection.*

Left, below: **Moon** *1987. Oil on canvas, 54 x 108 inches. Museum of Fine Arts, Houston, Collection.*

Above: **Tri-Emerge** *1993. Acrylic on canvas, 60 x 60 inches. Alton and Laurel Parks Collection.*

Page 165

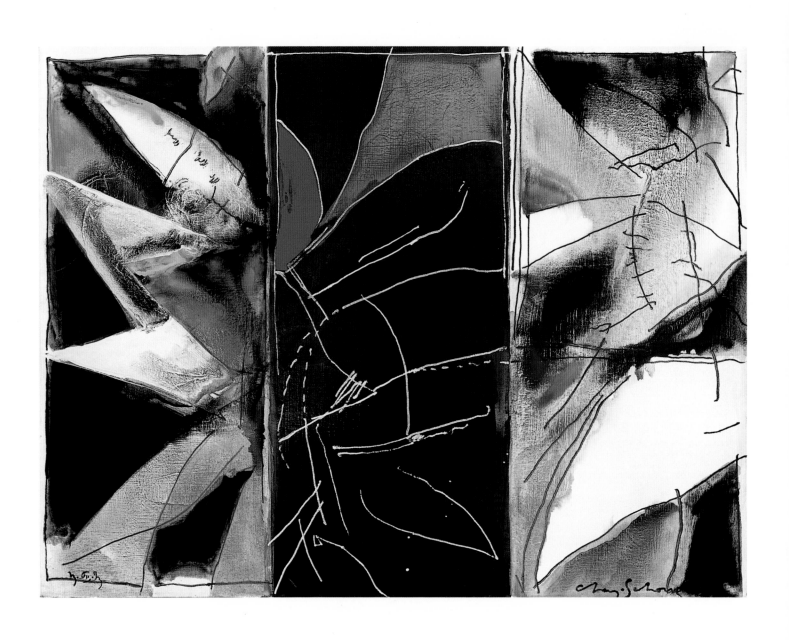

Above: **Triptych 93** *1993. Acrylic and oil on canvas, 36 x 48 inches. Artist's Collection.*

Right: **Mondrian's Culvert** *ND. Mixed-media collage on paper, 30 x 22 inches. Artist's Collection.*

p.B V 42)

Untitled *ND. Print, 18 x 22 inches. Laura Elizabeth Masquelette Collection.*

"I had been in Saudi Arabia and on my return,
met Miggie in Paris. We spent... time at
the Rodin Museum... and on the way out of
the garden entrance I made a film exposure.
The only one I made there. It was a faucet.
A freshly polished brass faucet. . . .

"A month later I was in Hunt, Texas... I had
spent the last week in the cabin by myself...
On the 2nd to last morning I got up and went
to the sink and saw the faucet in all its
glorious sunlight."

Faucet — Waltonia Lodge, Hunt, Texas; Faucet — Rodin Museum, Paris, France *ND. Mixed-media collage on paper, 20 x 30 inches.*
Lee and Carole Hamel Collection.

Page 169

Early Works

Above: **Church/Barn Landscape** *ND. Oil on masonite, 18 x 22 inches. Artist's Collection.*
Below, left: **Mission with Star** *ND. Acrylic on paper, 18½ x 24 inches. Annette Sanford Collection.*
Below, middle: **Shrimp Boat** *ND. Watercolor, 14 x 22½ inches. Annette Sanford Collection.*
Below, right: **Bend** *ND. Acrylic on canvas, 10½ x 14½ inches. Mary Barthlome Collection.*

Above: **Jim Glass Portrait** *1965. Oil and collage on canvas, 40 x 40 inches. Jim Glass Collection.*
Below, left: **Edward Steichen** *1961. Oil on canvas, 12 x 15 inches. Artist's Collection.*
Below, middle: **Untitled** *1967. Print, 13¾ x 18½ inches. Helen S. Morgan Collection.*
Below, right: **Dove** *1964. Print, 9½ x 11½ inches. Alton and Laurel Parks Collection.*

Page 171

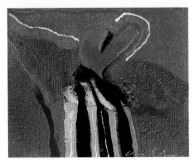

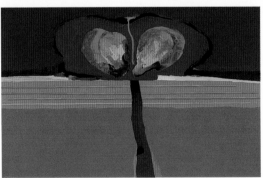

Above: **Dove** *1962. Oil on canvas, 40½ x 50½ inches. Lomis Slaughter Collection.*
Below, left: **Untitled** *ND. Acrylic and oil on canvas, 8 x 10 inches. Jack and Sharon Boynton Collection.*
Below, middle: **Mystic Meeting** *1970. Acrylic and oil on canvas, 42 x 66 inches. Barbara Eaves Collection.*
Below, right: **Autumnocturne** *1965. Oil on canvas, 8 x 10¼ inches. Miggie Schorre Collection.*

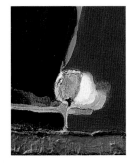   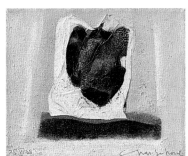

Above: **Love Bloom I** *1969. Oil on canvas, 36 x 36 inches. Lomis Slaughter Collection.*
Below, left: **Luna Bloom** *1967. Acrylic and oil on canvas, 10 x 8 inches. Artist's Collection.*
Below, middle (left): **Untitled** *1967. Acrylic on canvas, 10 x 8 inches. Helen S. Morgan Collection.*
Below, middle (right): **Untitled** *1968. Print, 10¼ x 13½ inches. Alton and Laurel Parks Collection.*
Below, right: **Dark Sign** *1968. Acrylic and oil on canvas, 8 x 10 inches. Artist's Collection.*

Page 173

Articles

A commitment to art
by Ivan Chermayeff
Pegasus, Issue 20, 1981

Ivan Chermayeff is director of the Mobil Arts Program and a designer of international stature.

Bedouin Cloud *1979. Print, 7¾ x 14 inches. Mobil Corporation Collection. (Not part of original article.)*

In World War II a tradition of visual recording, which probably dates to the Pharaohs, was maintained by the U.S. Government's establishment of a War Artists Program which sent individuals out to record their impressions in much the same way as recognized artists accompanied Victorian explorers or, still earlier, the campaigns of Napoleon.

The quality of communication transmitted by artists in their sketches of court trials, their travels into distant lands recorded in sketch books, the drawings and watercolors of botanists, archaeologists, zoologists, and other observers of the world around and beyond them have left us a poignant legacy.

In keeping with this tradition, Mobil has initiated an Artists-in-Residence program which allows a number of artists and photographers to express their own vision of Mobil's world.

The purposes of the program are several: to add color, warmth, and visual interest to Mobil offices, to foster a better understanding of contemporary art, and to support the arts communities and the best talents within them.

The policy of the art program is to place in public spaces — reception areas, waiting rooms, open office areas, corridors, and conference rooms — a wide range of artistic expression in all suitable media. This work, either purchased or commissioned, is to represent the best work within reasonable budget limitations.

The art program is not intended to be fixed or static. In all major facilities, where the corporate art program has been implemented, a pool of artwork will be housed to be available for rotation and from which employees may exchange work.

Six artists — three illustrators and three photographers — were asked to record their impressions of the worlds in which Mobil happens to operate. Each was given the assignment to go to an area, and, without restriction as to subject or form, capture some aspect of it they deemed relevant.

Charles Schorre, a painter, draftsman, and photographer, followed the pipeline from Jeddah across the Saudi Arabian peninsula, recording impressions of people from a past very much in the present. Later, in his Houston studio he assembled his photos and sketches into a series of collages combining abstraction and realism.

Robert Weaver, a skilled observer of sports and politics, people and places, spent weeks in Nigeria, around Lagos, along the coast and offshore amongst the oil platforms.

Daniel Schwartz, a master draftsman, traveled to the gas fields of Sumatra and the Harbor of Singapore, scene of Mobil's refinery, capturing the people, their old relationship to the land, and their new relationship to high technology.

Ron Scott, a young photographer from Houston, went down the Alaska pipeline to the Ferndale Refinery and saw the vast sweep of mountains, vistas, and lakes through which the pipeline passes.

Photographer Burke Uzzle spent time along the Gulf coast of Mexico from Morgan City to New Orleans and out on the Gulf itself recording the bayous, its architecture, and the oil world offshore.

Each of them submitted 100 works — drawings, watercolors, assemblages, or color photographs.

All the original work is now hanging in a number of Mobil facilities and the balance, not yet selected by Mobil employees, will eventually find homes in people's offices.

From the 600 original works produced for this first phase of the Artists-in-Residence a number were selected for limited reproduction, thus making an even greater number of works available for Mobil offices around the world. ■

To Remain in Doubt: An Interview with Charles Schorre

by James Bell and Lew Thomas
SPOT, Spring 1987

Painter, photographer, book designer, teacher, and former art director, Charles Schorre's paintings have been shown in the exhibitions *Fresh Paint* and *The Texas Landscape: 1900-1986* at the Museum of Fine Arts, Houston. The photography series *Pages From Books Unpublished* was exhibited at the Contemporary Arts Museum, Houston. His photographs were selected recently by Walter Hopps, director of The Menil Collection, for inclusion in *The Texas Annual* at the Laguna Gloria Museum, Austin, Texas. He is showing currently at the North Light Gallery in Tempe, Arizona in the exhibition *Five Houston Photographers.* Since the early sixties, Charles Schorre has produced several artist's books and has received numerous awards, grants, and an NEA Photo Fellowship.

You can easily see by this interview that what I'm about is disorientation. I used to be about orientation. . . direct orderly communication. . . now I'm about disorientation, mystery, polarity, sometimes confusion. . . questions instead of answers.

Q: We've come here to find some of the answers.

A: No answers, just a lot of questions.

Q: We're here to ask questions. We want to get some background, Charles. You started out in commercial art.

A: I started out. . . I have a degree in painting and sculpture from the University of Texas. I was exhibiting paintings in the *Texas General Exhibitions Annual* (Dallas, Houston, San Antonio Museum shows) before I graduated from the University of Texas. I got a job here in 1948 at the Museum of Fine Arts making 50 dollars a month teaching at night. My wife, Miggie, went to work, I painted. . . realized I'd have to do something so I got a job in an advertising agency where I learned how to draw and paint because I didn't learn rendering at the University. Later, I became a freelance art director, illustrator, graphic designer. I did a lot of art direction. . . I won awards and made a very good living. I won medals in New York and Europe for work I did for *Look* magazine, *Psychology Today, Playboy,* science fiction, Schlumberger, Hughes Tool,

all kinds of stuff. Lots of fun. Went on some trips. Then when I was teaching at Rice in the school of architecture, I did work for The National Institute of Mental Health about community mental hospitals. And that was really great. It was fun. I did some editing, some photography, some drawing. . . put two books together on community mental hospitals. At that time no one knew what they were. I consider everything I've ever done as part of my work. In Europe they don't separate much of it; unfortunately they separate too much here. Everything is categorized. Like if you're a photographer, how can you be a painter? And if you're a painter, how can you be a photographer? And if you're an art director or if you're an industrial designer, how can you have a photographic thought? I don't believe in that. So. That's about it.

Q: That's your career?

A: I got an ulcer in an advertising agency and, really, that's when I got out of organized labor. That was in the early sixties, late fifties. Didn't take long to get an ulcer in the advertising agency.

Q: You were successful. You won prizes.

A: Yeah, I won prizes as an art director, but as soon as I got out and started freelancing, that's when I really began winning awards in this country and some in Europe and got published in Japan, different things.

Q: You've always lived here in Texas?

A: Yeah, I was born in Cuero, Texas (9 March 1925). Came to Houston after graduating. I like the freedom this place gives me.

Q: Houston?

A: Yeah, lots of freedom. I don't have to run off to see a lot of shows. If I were in New York, I'd run myself to death. I don't know what I'd be. I have a great interest in jazz. . . I might not be alive if I lived in New York. I also wanted to maintain a family and we are doing that. We have three daughters and seven grandchildren. I'm just a very close family person.

Q: You spent some time in the Marine Corps.

A: I was in the Marine Corps for 3½ years . . . but I'm really a pacifist now. I was stationed on Guam. . . all the action I saw was accidental. . . people coming out of the jungle, not knowing the war was over. I was a sergeant in the infantry. I became angry when I was still at the OCS in Quantico and lost my commission. . . had a fight with a colonel. That probably kept me from being killed. My being sent overseas was delayed. I believe in capital punishment, but I don't believe in war. I believe that if you high-jack a plane and threaten people maybe you

ought to be shot on the way out of the plane. Since I was in Saudi Arabia I believe that. Because I could put my camera and sketchbooks down on any street corner and come back and pick them up the next day.

Q: Because. . .

A: They would cut off your arm for stealing. But that's not the only thing I liked over there. I loved the desert, and the huge contrasts and conflicts of moral and religious and industrial interests. You felt like you were in Jesus' time on one corner and then on the next corner you felt like you were in Europe. So that was a wonderful influence being there. Very strong, intense. Like taking a real strong pill for a month. I just had a month, but I stayed awake most of the time.

Q: Did it have anything to do with the intensity of color?

A: Actually, less. It was all sand and sand-blasted automobiles and rust. In the desert you don't see anything but the white male costume or the black female dress. And rust . . . everything was very camouflaged. Dirty. The only colors were Pepsi bottles, trash thrown out of automobiles, tin cans that wouldn't rust. Except in the city where you had the garish contemporary architecture which is a little bit of everything. There's one beautiful campus in Dhahran. . . The minerals and petroleum university. . . a friend of mine from Houston designed it. And the Saudis are real proud of it. They think they did it. I love the country, though, and the peasant people. You could be closer to the women and the men in the rural areas where in the city everybody was sort of paranoid. . . and you were not allowed conversation with women. Saudi Arabia was like one huge unfinished painting. . . I guess that is my main reason for loving it. . . just a big piece of unfinished art.

Q: You went over there on an exchange basis?

A: No, a Mobil Oil artist in residence grant from New York. It came out of the blue. I didn't apply for it or anything. It just showed up.

Q: Great!

A: Yeah, it was really a shock. I got a National Endowment grant as soon as I got back and I thought it was a joke.

Q: When did you receive the grant?

A: I think it was the latter part of '79.

Q: For a photo fellowship?

A: Yeah, it was one of their large grants. For the *Pages* that I'm doing now.

Q: So what was the date when you made the commitment to pursue your personal art?

A: I've always pursued my personal art, but getting an ulcer allowed me full time

 Reprinted with permission: Originally appeared in SPOT (Volume V, Number 1), a publication of Houston Center for Photography, copyright 1986.

devotion. I was really learning how to draw in this advertising agency. I learned about color. I also learned to photograph because I was in the bullpen, they called it, and I was sent out on the oil rigs with a Speedgraphic to shoot what they called round trips for Hughes Tool rock bits. And I shot photographic information for other illustrators who were better than I. I didn't know how to use the Speedgraphic and they taught me. I'd go out and sometimes spend all night on an oil rig. But that really laid a foundation for what I'm doing now. I really learned how to see with a camera. My first camera was a Rolleicord. I had some work during 1956 and 1957 in *Popular Photography Annuals*, my straight photographs. And *Creative Camera* was another one and so I was doing photography and painting all the time. I was either painting or photographing and I saw that by taking the photographs I could integrate the two. I started out as a realist and became abstract. The birth/death or the life/death series that I'm actually still working on, the constant conflict and the closeness of life and death, that started in the early fifties, soon after Miggie and I got married. The series was also started by ecumenical church activity, by meeting Paul Tillich and reading Kierkegaard and different people like that. I realize that although I'm an attempted Christian I really have never read the Bible and probably never will. I mean in its entirety. Even if I did I probably wouldn't think much differently than I do right now. So. . . I met a lot of people and when I did the Bishop Pike book for *Look* magazine there were several people in the book that I already knew. They were personal friends and still are.

Q: You seem to identify the "life/death" business with the different ways you use art, the painting and the photography.

A: Yeah? I think it's the polarity. . . the seesawing, the tension between light and dark and realism and abstraction, ecstasy and discovery. I believe in this tension. If I started a series that I would really enjoy and it would catch on and people started buying it, I would stop. I would just literally stop.

Q: You'd stop producing that kind of work because. . .

A: It would also be boring. I need the money and sometimes I'm desperate for money, but I don't paint for money. I paint for discovery. I mean, wow, gee whiz. I never have done that sort of thing before. . . for the awe of it.

Q: Because of the polarity between photography and painting?

A: Absolutely. I know it's imagined, but I think it's real too. A lot of painters don't

want to get near photography or they don't want to use it or manipulate it, and I think people like Warhol and, well, even Picasso. . . any kind of collage work gives us permission to use anything. In my collage work, I like to use my own material. When I taught collage at the museum several years ago, I wanted my students to use their own material. I think it's more difficult and more edgy to tear up your own material than to use the printed matter of someone else.

Q: So you're relying on your own content and material to create these collages rather than appropriate from other sources.

A: But I don't sit down and say I'm going to manufacture some collage material. It's just residue from other work I do. I mean I've got stacks and stacks of material. You can imagine. 'Cause I like to produce and I'm a very tight critic. My wife's the best critic I've ever seen. She's ruthless. So I also destroy a lot of stuff.

Q: Does she have an art background?

A: No! But she is a natural. . . has what I'd call a perfect eye and feeling for relevance in visual and conceptual work. All this is native to Miggie.

Q: Can you give us an example of how that operates in a particular case?

A: Okay. I can take three paintings in the room there and put them on the wall. Three different paintings, mine or someone else's; it doesn't make any difference. And I'll come back in there and if she's rearranged them it's obvious that's where they belong. Theme wise or value wise or size wise. . . it would even have all the wit and humor that things juxtaposed have.

Q: Were you pleased with your show at Meredith Long?

A: Very pleased. I was not pleased that I didn't have the whole gallery. I had to cut the show down. I have a show every two years. So I did a lot of changing at the last minute. But I was very pleased with the way it came out.

Q: What do you mean by being pleased?

A: I liked what I had up and I liked the response of people. I got some surprise feedback from people I consider to be good critics and I got some super feedback from some buyers and from some people who said they didn't know anything about art. They responded to the contrast of the work.

Asked me questions about the black paintings, they called them. These things were no-nonsense questions, they were serious. When I can get that kind of variety, I believe that's fine. I'm really not trying to communicate with anyone. But if someone gets something out of the work that they can tell me about, that's what I really love. I worked

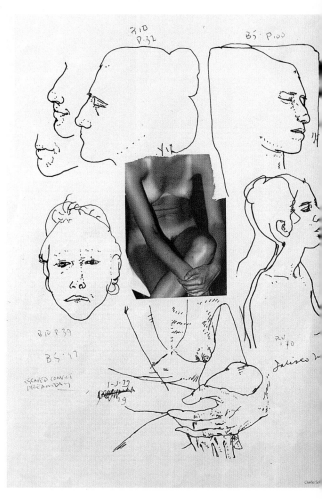

Pages From Books Unpublished #137 *ND.*
(Shown in original article.)

so long being a communicator that I'm not trying to sell a message anymore. That's always troublesome for the public, to think that artists are not primarily into communication. Many people find that a contradiction.

Q: If you're not into communication, what are you doing? Creating something original?

A: I would rather try to make some mark for the spirit, the soul, the silent nature or allness of a thing than to reproduce the obvious noise of a thing. When I was an illustrator, I was sometimes reproducing the obvious noise of something. I might be saying, "Dammit, this is it and I want to hit you over the head with it." I'm not doing that now; I'm exploiting myself instead of other people.

Q: The artist should exploit him or herself?

A: Yes. If it's a housewife or a computer operator or anyone, I'm saying exploit yourself. If you start looking inward instead of outward for signs, then you'll see your own sign and your own directions and you can move. You might move into areas you never dreamed of.

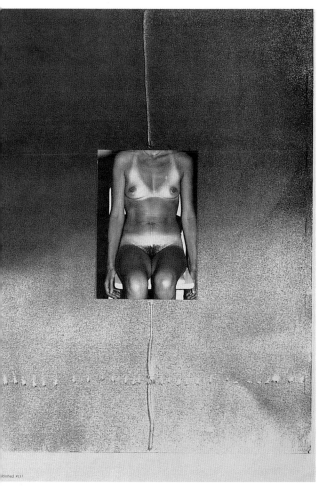

Photographs, drawing on board, no size given. Artist's Collection.

Q: You're a real intense guy.

A: I've had some friends who've committed suicide, young and old. And I believe if you want to say something, for God's sake say it. But don't wait for the proper time because there is no proper time.

Q: Is this a personal philosophy, or have you developed it from readings?

A: I don't say it's the answer for anybody. If you want to "get ahead," it's not the answer. It's my answer. I'm not saying I have an answer for anything. Because the reward is no reward, the answer is no answer. This is just the way I feel. For instance, right now I have no concept of whether it's morning or afternoon or Monday or Tuesday or Wednesday. I'm in no hurry to go anywhere; we are doing this interview. I've actually gotten into my own

automobile into the back seat and wondered who was going to drop me off. Everybody does those things, but I realize that you can really get into some kind of horrible accident that might even be a life and death situation by not being present.

Q: You'd better tell us that again, Charles.

A: Okay, I'll tell you. . . if you're driving an automobile, for instance, and really not driving the automobile. That's dangerous. Or there's a humor thing. You want to be at your place of work and you've got two kids to take to a movie that morning. It's cold and raining, and you've got to urinate, and you're in a line with thirty people. But you're thinking about work, and you get up to the ticket booth, and he asks how many and you open your raincoat and unzip instead of giving the guy the money. Now that's a humorous example. But you can do that in a dangerous situation where it's an automobile or an airplane. Or by not being present or alert when you're on a highway or walking across a street or in your own work.

Q: And you feel that way about your work?

A: I feel that way. Right now, doing this interview is the most important thing. . . I'm not painting . . . I'm giving this my full attention, believe it or not. But you can easily see that what I might be about is disorientation. I used to be about orientation. . . orderly, "to the point" headline communication. . . Now I'm about mystery, polarity, sometimes even confusion. . . questions instead of answers.

Q: That's the way your art looks. It has a kind of gestural intensity.

A: Well, I appreciate that. I hope it has.

Q: There's a physicality to it.

A: I hope there is.

Q: That's important to you?

A: Oh, it is. . . I love beautiful photographs but God, you can bore yourself to death, become guilty of visual/creative suicide looking at beautiful photographs.

Q: Do you consciously push yourself towards awkwardness in order to reach some other edge of meaning or experience or aesthetics?

A: That's true. I don't like being so awkward that it's ugly art on purpose, ugly drawing, or what I call inept. Because I have a facility and I don't want to betray that facility. So I like to juxtapose photographs and paintings because they don't belong

together. The surfaces are different and if you don't believe me, if you're a painter and have never collaged a photograph in the middle of your pretty painting, try it sometime. It's just hell to work out.

Q: The issue of awkwardness and intensity is obvious in your work. On the other hand, you seem to rely on the language of cubism as a compositional device.

A: Hmmm. I didn't know that.

Q: The use of planes, organizing from the level of the two-dimensional plane in order to set up your contradictions.

A: Contradictions?

Q: Well, your contradictions, your messages, the signs expressed in your paintings and collages even though you say you're not a communicator. And there's a flatness to some of the work. It seems to me that you're coming out of a cubistic tradition. Your references to Picasso. . .

A: Hmmm. Yeah.

Q: You reference the masters in a number of your pieces.

A: Yeah, I guess I do. Matisse and Cézanne and Rodin and Gorky and Gauguin. . . yeah. But *Gorky and His Mother.* I think that's one of the finest paintings of this century. Because it's unfinished. That's why I like Stuart's *George Washington,* because the damn thing's unfinished. It brings in, in a very simplistic way, the viewer. He's actually on board, because he tries to finish that painting every time he looks at it.

Q: You sound like Duchamp.

A: Yeah, I believe in that.

Q: It's also a postmodern position, come to think of it, because the reader has become influential in making the decision about experiencing art. The viewer, the reader, has to make a commitment.

A: I believe that when I finish a painting, it's half done. And if others attach themselves to it, they have an opportunity to finish it. If they buy it and look at it for a long time, I hope they get messages out of it for a long time. It's like an open-ended story. It continues. That's why I like going on a trip. A trip extends itself. You think about it a lot. That's why I like drawings.

Q: The trip is fresh?

A: Yeah, the trip is fresh. You've got that trip on your back. That's why I like drawings, because a drawing is a shorthand of something, yet it's just as abstract as you can get. That's why I say good realism is abstract and good abstraction is realism. I get the message pretty fast if it's a realistic piece. But if it's a super-realistic piece, a real piece of art, I can sit there and get as much from it as from an abstraction. I'm still trying to look at something and see it like I've never seen it before, and that extends its presence.

Q: You don't think you're perpetuating stereotypes?

A: No, absolutely not. I might be doing the opposite.

Q: By creating it so that it looks fresh?

A: Yes. Different. I used to go to different places in my backyard when we had a big yard. One time I went and sat up on top of the air-conditioning unit. Or under a table. I just believe that our expectations are so strong that we live our expectations and sometimes they have nothing to do with reality. Repent, turn yourself around.

Q: Can you tell us about your methodologies. Do you have a different methodology for painting in contrast to photography? Do you work in a series? Do you work on four or five things at the same time?

A: Sometimes six or seven. I work on the *Hand* series like that, whenever it occurs to me. That's something I know that's there and I can go to it. The hand stuff. . .

Q: It's an ongoing project?

A: Yeah, it's ongoing. I have over three hundred of these, same with *Pages From Books Unpublished,* close to four hundred now.

Q: The collage photographs?

A: They're slowly getting into the bigger paintings. The *Artist's Handbook* series and *Pages From Books Unpublished* are two series that have been going on for a long time. And this life/death stuff has been going on for a long time. But along with all this other work, some short stories have come. I've got about three or four. One science fiction and some straight pieces. All of a sudden. I'll sit down there drinking coffee and it'll be like those bone drawings up there. That's what I call them. That's how they came. One afternoon, after a nap, they were all in a sketchbook and I transferred them to handmade paper. The only way I could possibly reach those is through solitude.

Q: The resume said that around 1970 you really separated yourself from a lot of professional organizations and societies. What was that all about?

A: It was a way of gaining time. The only way I could do it was to just do it all at once.

Q: So it wasn't anything personal you had against those particular societies?

A: Yeah, it was a protest too, against things like the American Watercolor Society, juried shows, invitational shows, any kind of organization. I just got fed up.

Q: The other thing I've observed or think I've observed about your work is that I can sort of see the progression that you've made going from the graphic arts and the illustra-

tor background to something that seems to be just a commitment made to your personal expression of things or your intuition of things. And I wanted to ask you if it's as much of a progression as I think it is. You started doing artists' books like *Pages From Books Unpublished* and you incorporated photography in a lot of your work. But in some of your recent work that was in the gallery you do not incorporate photography. It's a total painting. Is that what you're moving toward?

A: No, I don't really think that way. The only way I can see trails is to look back at my slide collection, pull it out as an intuitive, unintentional thing. I don't organize, like come in today and say, I'm working on this and by the end of the year I should have this or this. I want it to be sort of out of control. I want it to be as out of control as I can get it without losing touch with it. I want to be totally aware of what I'm doing. I want to be totally aware of the manipulation but I want it to be out of control.

Q: Right. But you don't think you've drawn upon your background?

A: I've deliberately drawn upon everything I have available. Other than having somebody play a saxophone by one of my paintings. I just cut off music, the participating in the playing of music, because it's a different thing.

Q: So those things you were involved with in the past as a professional are serving you.

A: It's all a part of me. Christianity is a part of me. Any kind of spiritual activity is very, very important to me. The silent language is very, very important to me. Your interpretation of what happened is great. That's what I like about the silent language bit. Because you don't have my words, you have your own feelings. It's like being in love. That's what it is.

Q: How do you view the photograph in relation to an entire piece. Sometimes you'll be working on a painting and you'll just see a photograph and it just seems to fit. Is it really that haphazard?

A: Yeah, it is. I use a photograph as a hammer or a brush. Only it's more of a complete thing, more of a mechanical thing. It's a tool. It's like a computer in a way. It's something

I can use. And I'm not afraid of it. Like Thelonious Monk said one time, "I play stuff I didn't even know I could play." That's what I'd like to do, just go, "Gosh, did I do that?" Not just to amaze myself, but that's part of waking up.

Q: Then one starts to work with and against the other?

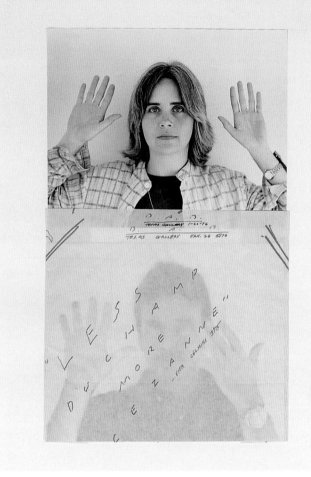

Pages From Books Unpublished-Gallery Owners *1977.*
(Not part of original article.)

A: Yeah, they start talking to each other. They start going with each other.

Q: One of the issues in your work, and it's something that came up recently at the Center [The Houston Center for Photography] because of the Patrick Clancy installation, has to do with accessibility. Looking at your work, photography seems to be a key in some way to gain access to the painting. Have you heard that before or thought about it yourself?

A: I haven't heard it before and have not thought about it, but that's very good. I believe that. I believe that's true. It also could be a key for someone turning off the whole thing.

Q: Aside from the fact that it's an applied object that's going to change in some way, visually, the image, the photographic element seems to open a door into the rest of the piece.

A: It opens a door, but I can also say the same for the painted part. It might open a door to the photograph.

Q: So you're really working one with the other?

A: Yeah, they're seesawing. And I don't

Photographs on illustration board, 22 x 30 inches. Museum of Fine Arts, Houston, Collection.

want one to gain power over the other. That paint is not a background for that photograph. But sometimes it becomes so. And if it works, I leave it. But most of them are not backgrounds, they are well-integrated, they are juxtaposed parts. . . they interlock.

Q: Why do you feel the need to push it beyond that one surface?

A: Because the other would be too easy for me. There's another thing I want to say about the photo. I wish more than once a week that I did straight photographs and they sold and I could go to the negative and make another one. I wish that. I cannot do that with these pieces. There's no way that I can repeat them. I wish more than once a week that I did, like a lot of friends of mine, straight, even sports' paintings. . . and had people waiting in line for the paintings and I

could charge big prices for them. I wish that at times. But then I say, I can't do that. I could do it, but I might go crazy in about five years, just go strictly bats. I mean, never come back. I'm having too much intriguing fun. I can go into this studio space, which is very crowded, but I can go into this space sick or well or any time of day or night and wander around in here and get attached to something. I'm not bored in here. I've got a million things I want to do in here. That's the reason I don't travel as much anymore.

Q: You've created your own world in the studio?

A: Like Rothko going through "his own museum," he called it, seeing his own stuff on people's walls. Someone else called it that, Picasso, I think. I use the slides as a vehicle to go through my own museum. I did a lecture on the eighth of January and just getting a little slide tray together for that particular time, 20 minutes or 30 minutes, caused me to go through my museum. And then I deliberately ask, "What are you going to say that might be valid to those people?"

Q: What would you like to say, Charles, without the interference of questions? Your point of view, Charles.

A: I would like to go back and say what I said when we started. Whether you're young or old or just starting out or even consider yourself a professional, if you aren't following your own voice, silent voices or whatever, your own feelings, if you've never tapped your own voice as the source, I think you're really gypping yourself. . . even if you're a twin, there's something unique about you in particular. And there's something you can do with that as an artist.

Q: What can you suggest to someone who doesn't have financial independence or the. . . freedom. . . it's a little tougher, perhaps. . .

A: Start grabbing 5, 10, 15 minutes a day, like you're writing a book. Like you go to the bathroom, like you spend the time to eat, like you watch TV. Just a little each day. And call it your own, in a chamber, someplace where you can go quietly and sit down. . . let's say you're writing a book or let's say you're doing an eight-foot square painting. If you put 15 minutes for 365 days on that canvas, you're going to be through

with it in a year. You might even be through with it six months from now. You're starting. . . you can't eat the whole thing at once. I mean, you've got an elephant to devour there and there's no need to say, "I gotta eat that sonofabitch tonight." But start finding . . . keeping a daybook and asking. . . even interviewing yourself. And finding what's going on inside of you. Why do you hate so-and-so? Why are you here? What brings you here — the money or the ecstasy or, you know, what the hell are you doing? Or what do you really want to do? Do you really want to make a lot of money for one year and jam it down someone's throat. . . and then get on with your life?

Q: Now you've talked about your daybooks before.

A: Yeah, the daybooks. Now, I never believed in daybooks. I told the students to use them but until about. . . oh, I guess ten years ago, I started using them. And. . . they're all over the place . . . my encyclopedia of me.

Q: And you just go back to them at random sometimes?

A: I go back to them as reference. For instance, if our anniversary comes up, I'll go back in the index and see if I've written anything about that. A poem — I'm not a poet, but I've got some poems in there. Any kind of new vision you can get or any kind of new feeling you can get. . . that's why I like the Center so much. Every time I go over there, there's something new. But I don't give it that much time because I'm anxious to get back here. So it's really a source place. And that's what I like about making yourself your own source place.

Q: You seem very positive about Houston. You know, when we first started the interview, you spoke of the freedom here.

A: Yeah, I. . . I have the freedom here. . . it's in kind of a negative way. I couldn't work in Aspen or Guadalajara or anyplace in Europe where the scenery's really great.

Q: Well, how about the dialogue that exists in a place like Houston? Is it adequate for you?

A: Plenty adequate, yeah. The support system is weak. That is what I really feel bad about. There's little courageous collecting going on. There are a few pockets of collecting and thank God for that.

Q: Do you want to be specific about the . . .

A: I really can't. But I know that I've been fortunate. I know also that I could count three people that I could call really, true collectors who buy. . . have large collections of my work. But gosh, that's nothing. In New

York if you had three, well, maybe that's all you need. The only thing I see where anyone exerts any large amount of money is in cowboy art or sports or something like that . . . and it's unfortunate.

Q: The institutions contribute to that?

A: I think the institutions can be as guilty as any of us. I think we all contribute to it. But I think the institutions are locked up as tight as a drum.

Q: The alternative spaces are active. They support experimental art.

A: Yeah, and it's getting better. . . there's really a lot happening here.

Q: How about the area of publication?

A: It's better than it was. You can't just go out and publish a book. But there are a lot of people living here who are writers and photographers that do have their stuff published. So it's getting better.

Q: Is there a lot of interactiveness among these different groups, like writers and painters and dancers?

A: I don't know. . . haven't invested enough time.

Q: What about the level of criticism here?

A: Very sad. . . it's always been an "up for grabs" wasteland, but it seems to be getting better. . . people out there making some discoveries for themselves, getting some courage. . . it is moving along in slow motion. Critics need support also in order to do what they do.

Q: The schools?

A: Well, we're regional.

Q: How do you feel about the universities here, their art departments. Do you feel like they're fairly strong?

A: No, I really don't, but then again I have not given them enough time to really know what's going on. If art was making news in the universities, it would be hard to avoid.

Q: Then you have the other schools like Glassell.

A: I think that they're improving and they've got their own curatorial thing now for shows and they're doing better. I think it's very healthy looking. There's more life in the art community now. If it weren't, I wouldn't be here. You're here. Why are you here?

Q: Yeah, there are some gaps in the structure here that make it possible for people to create work I believe would be more difficult to do in other cities.

A: In a locked up city. You hit the key to why I think I might be here. There are some gaps and those gaps open things up. Now, this is what I like about it. Because those holes and those voids, those places, those hard times cause people to be very innova-

tive. I think there are a lot of good signs. That's why I started spouting out at Diverse Works a year ago, or a year and a half or two years ago. I happened to be at a little open forum. There were not many people there, but I just started spouting out. And using HCP [Houston Center for Photography] as an example of somebody doing a publication, somebody doing something that's beyond regionalism. I'm not saying they followed my advice or anything but look what's happened down there.

Q: You're pleased with the way Diverse Works has developed?

A: Yeah. I mean, it's exciting. They're doing things that people haven't thought of. I'm sorry they're not closer by. I'd like to walk over there every afternoon. But the point is that it's getting done. Sure you do a lot of things that don't work, but you do the workable, too. I still hold SPOT up as a shining example. I mean it. And I don't care whether you agree with that particular issue or don't agree with it. It's not just regional. And that's mainly what I'm interested in. I'm not a regional painter, but I'm classified as a regional painter. I don't do cowboys.

Q: Do you think the opening of The Menil Collection will bring some added. . .

A: Oh, it's going to be fantastic. I mean, that's a monumental situation. No one can compete with that. And the fallout from that is going to be glorious. It's going to put everybody into a competitive spirit. It's going to excite the other institutions. The main thing that's happened this last year is the interchange between Diverse Works and HCP. That didn't exist before.

Q: Do you think it's necessary for the younger artists in Houston to build a network among themselves for showing their work, writing about it?

A: They're barracudas. Now it's barracuda-ville. You talk about network and that's all they think about. That's just like the yuppies. They don't think about protesting on a campus or supporting that, they're out there making money and putting it in a box. I think in a way it's just real tragic. But yes, you have to network now to survive.

Q: What do you recommend the artist pursue?

A: Work. There's no doubt about it. . . what we do is work. I have a lot of friends who are highly talented but they don't have the passion. And they're still wondering what's happened to them. And nothing will ever happen to them. They're dilettantes.

Q: Do you have any recommendations for the Center or SPOT? What do you think are its strong points, its weaknesses?

A: I really don't know what they are. And

I don't know what is really the strongest point. I think the sustenance, the continuation of SPOT is more important to me because you're going to have some issues that bomb and some that are unique if you're experimenting at all. And I think you should experiment.

Q: In what way?

A: In a literary way and a visual way. Both ways. The way you did in the last issue, use valid letters to the editor. Because there was something going on there. And it extended the article.

Q: Unfortunately it's not easy to get the letters.

A: Well, one of the things we might do is get some feedback from New York, San Francisco, or L.A. and really get some hard criticism. Ask for it. The way you're asking for it from me. But I'm so close to it. . . I just want it to continue. I just love seeing that thing happen. And once it stops I'm going to be very disappointed. I hate to say it, it might be even more important than the exhibits. Because it's still sitting there after the exhibit leaves. I think another thing that the Center could do and should do as quickly as possible, if they have to steal to do it, is get some audio visual equipment for the speakers who come through here. We're missing a fantastic opportunity. We ought to have a library of videotapes. But I like the Center because I'm really not a photographer or a painter. I'm a person over there. I don't threaten anyone. I may do it, but I'm not aware of it. And if I do I don't intend to threaten anyone. I just want to pick somebody up every now and then, including myself. But I think the Center, just like Diverse Works, is doing a very valid thing. It's doing it on eggshells. It's not doing it on any solid foundation at all. Isn't that right? And when you're doing stuff on eggshells, you're doing a dance. I mean, you're really doing a highly creative dance that might explode anytime and you might disappear. Just vanish. Gone. There just has to be some hope.

Q: There are very few people out there where you are.

A: I can't be there all the time but I'm aware of that position when I'm fearless. And I'm in the other position when I'm devastated too, just scared to death. I mean, where I feel like I have no control over the situation. And I really feel sorry for someone who says, "Oh I want to be an artist," and they really don't have any passion. I'm not talking about having the facility or the vehicle. You don't have to draw to get there. You don't need to even know how to use a camera to get there. ■

Review

Paintings by Charles Schorre: Colors burst forth on minds set free

by Carol Everingham
The Houston Post, December 18, 1983

Experience number one, from Charles Schorre's book *Life Class*:

Look at things as if for the very first time,
as if you had been blind,
and, suddenly, could see.

Colors. Pure, raw, envigorating blues, oranges, yellows burst forth on the canvases of Charles Schorre. Space comes alive with an energy and intensity of coals rather than a brush fire. His yellows are as vivid as a sunflower, his violets are cool and collected.

But it is his blue—cosmic, ultramarine blue—which contains the mystery. Not exactly the *Chartres bleu* of medieval stained glass, nor the modern presence of an Yves Klein international blue. Schorre's blue is the only one of its kind in acrylic. And he ages it!

Re-envision the commonplace,
the sights you have looked at so often
and no longer "see."

See how the sun rises and the day changes. *Daychange II* becomes almost a continental map of a new dawn or dusk. Between an upper and lower horizon line, the roses and fresh blues rush in, separating the deep purple from the virtually virgin white void. It is like a breath of fresh air.

Look at things as though you do not
know what you are looking at.
Look at things as though you were
an insect.

Watch the wings of *Insectsong I* and *II* glitter with a sun/moon dust that glide by in golden splendor. Feel the airiness of dynamic color being transported through space.

Schorre does this to you. He makes you stop, look and listen to a whole new vocabulary of motion, depth and cosmic highs. At 58, Schorre is as stimulating as ever. His paintings and drawings (on exhibition at DuBose Gallery, 2950 Kirby Drive) are to be experienced by letting the mind go free, giving imagination the reins and rationality a rest.

As in a peek into his now-completed architectural course at Rice University, Schorre offers an opportunity to take a breather from the complex figurative or heavy abstractness of so-called Modern art. In a series of 14 recent paintings and 40 "unpublished" drawings, Schorre allows a sort of meditative energy to pour forth, defying the abstract by giving it form.

Look at things as though you were. . .
30,000 feet tall.
Do this without a crutch of any kind—
except your fully alerted self.

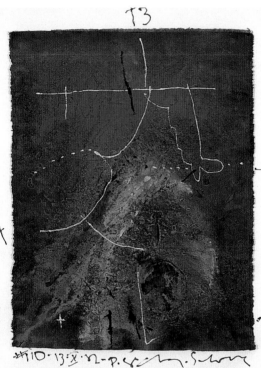

1+2+3=10 *1982. Collage, oil, and acrylic, 25½ x 19½ inches. Joe Colangelo Collection. (Shown in original article.)*

Experience a six-mile high and witness a *Moonavel* — with a belly button to boot. Galaxies of stars become the motifs of exploration. *Stardance* does just that; *Three-track Stardance* consist of trios of stars that waltz from line to line in the ecstasy of life. Other stars from *Pages From Books Unpublished* soar through space with blazing tails of comets or walk away from shadows.

Schorre is a master of the uninhibited line. His lines dance with glee, or skip into provocative shapes, such as the skull outline *Dead Queenmother Attempting to Give Her Dying King Son His Final Signal*. Her message is there, somewhere, trying desperately to be communicated. *Two Silly Girls Teasing a Freak Animal* and *Running Oasis With Young Palm* could really be nothing else. Schorre describes this series of "nature traces" and "human marks" as impressions made one afternoon drinking a cup of coffee after a mid-day nap. The titles came the following day.

But isn't this what art is all about? Spontaneity, vivid and refreshing?

Schorre brings together worlds that are seemingly far apart. His "nature traces" are evocative of prehistoric cave paintings, visions of the hunted and the chased, the haunted and the chaste. Sensuous lines are disciplined, yet loose and playful. At the other end of the spectrum is the space-age cosmic quality of outer realms. With laser sharpness, lines are etched and recorded into uncharted, unframed planes. Like a pioneer on a solo mission, Schorre explores the unconscious, exhilarating sensations of inner sanctums of the creative mind.

And it could only happen in Houston, he says, because the lack of visual stimulus outside (except for architecture) entices visions of other imaginary worlds. Aspen is overkill; New England is too perfect. Inspiration must come from within.

Schorre has remained faithful to his Houston environment and the intimacy of his small studio near Morningside and Sunset. One of Ben DuBose's original five artists, Schorre has commandeered a new generation of explorers to ask their own questions, to describe what they see with their own personal vocabulary. As Schorre defines it: "My paintings are dialogues" — travelogues of altitudes, attitudes and states of being an artist.

Whether it be the *Powerplay* of two great pyramids, or the strength of *Godsthumb* diagonal digits crisscrossing a polarized star center, Schorre's universe is keeping time with the music of the spheres.

And it could just as appropriately have been a phone call to his studio — instead of the one once made to Yves Klein's — by an excited friend reporting Yuri Gagarin's first comments from orbit:

The machines are working normally,
I can see the earth
Space is black
The earth is blue
I'm going on with the flight.

It must have been that Schorre blue. ∎

Charles Schorre

by Dugald Stermer
Communication Arts Magazine,
Vol. 9, No. 2, 1967

Religious art? Now? You're putting me on.

Religious art simply died of old age and overexposure sometime between the latter part of the seventeenth century and the early part of the nineteenth.

Charles Schorre: "If I have to go back into history to have my religious experience, I cannot have one. Someone else, living in that time and that place, has already had it for me. An historical event, misused as personal involvement, is adult thumb-sucking."

There have been, and still are, a few spiritual throwbacks in art — Georges Roualt, Marc Chagall, even Salvadore Dali; and the somewhat lesser known Sister Mary Corita and John Paul Jones. And, of course, Charles Schorre.

Although he would admit of no such categorical distinctions, Schorre is an instructor of life drawing at Rice University in Houston, an art director, illustrator, designer, photographer and most certainly a painter. A "religious" painter.

Schorre: "Recently about fourteen of my paintings were on exhibit at Rice University. Because they were religious paintings no 'art authority' would commit himself in print about the exhibition. It was, however, exciting to discover a great number of people, who weren't particularly educated about art, accepting a Kennedy assassination painting, a heart painting, a love painting, a birth painting and a landscape in a 'religious art' show."

The predominant symbol in the great body of Schorre's work is the cruciform; but that isn't saying much by itself. He takes the subject and bends it, tears it open, shapes it, sometimes only hints at it. He turns it into a womb, or a bird, or a heart. Occasionally he combines many of these forms in one painting, using superb draughtmanship to weave these elements into the one Christ figure.

Schorre: "Some of these things became real for me while working, since 1960, on a theme of crucifixion-birth. . . life-death. . . to die to become. . . stop, turn around, go again, live again. . . in another direction."

His involvement is total and thorough. He brings a full set of skills to everything he does: drawing, photography, design and art direction (he has an intuitive sense of typography).

A man with few noticeable inhibitions, Schorre is, in the opinion of some of his local colleagues, somewhat of a nut.

Honesty, complete open personal honesty, is nearly always embarrassing, perhaps because we come upon it so seldom and just don't know how to handle it.

Schorre: "If this historical happening is your only religious experience, you can't be blamed if someone 'proves' that it didn't happen. You can't be blamed for not having the guts to have your own religious experience. You might be afraid that it might be 'out,' or 'camp,' the wrong thing to do that year, just as Christ's being on the cross was the wrong thing to do that other year."

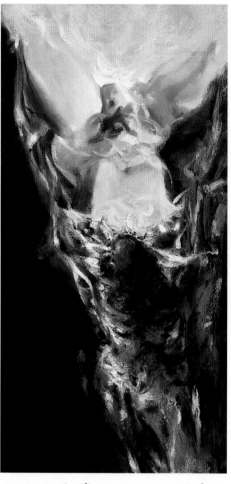

Untitled *ND. Acrylic on canvas, 36 x 18 inches. Jane H. Gregory Collection. (Not shown in original article, but very similiar to images included in original article.)*

Although we have been friends for a few years now, I received a new insight into Schorre's character just this past June at the conclusion of the Aspen Design Conference. It was after a two hour lunch with Charles, another friend and his wife, and myself. As we were leaving the table the friend came up to me, pulled me aside and said, "You know, what that guy just said made more sense to me than anything I've heard all week. He knows who he is."

———

Schorre has been a consistent award winner in the Society of Illustrators exhibitions. A medal winner in the latest show, he was invited to address the awards dinner last January. The following is excerpted from that speech:

I live and work a long way away — in Houston. So perhaps I look at the Society with a different perspective than you do. Maybe my view is a little rural, but I also believe it's a little easier for me to see the whole landscape of the Society of Illustrators more clearly from where I sit than you do close up. It's easier for me to see and admire — or not to admire — the masses of trees in this detailed landscape instead of all the little leaves.

For the Society not to have a superbly displayed exhibition each year is a disgrace. But it's a disgrace that's inevitable in our present frame of mind. When you think of it, it's amazing that this show ever gets up. Just nailing this many nails in the wall so close together takes a helluva lot of time and energy. And did it ever occur to you that it's curious that we, who are in the business of communication, don't include the complete printed piece beside the original art so people can see what it's all about?

It's time we think deeply about our reason for being. Are we necessary? I think we are. But are we the *living end* the way the illustrator used to be? I don't think so. We could learn a lot from these fellows that used to be the *living end*, though, and I think we'd be a lot better off.

It used to be that the illustrator handled "art directing and everything." Then, after a while, he became a specialist in made-by-hand pictures and left "art directing and everything" to others. About that time, one of the greatest visual communicators of all time came to age: photography.

As illustrators, some of us tried to kid ourselves that this was a fad we'd have to ride out. Like blacksmiths and buggywhip manufacturers, the "I-make-pictures-by-hand" illustrators refused to admit that these other fellows were here to stay.

We're getting to be like the blacksmiths with no more horses to put shoes on. It's time for us to figure out what the hell we're going to do with those red hot shoes before they freeze dark on us. In some ways we're lucky; we've got the time to refire — the metal is still good and so is our muscle. But the fact remains — we're short on horses.

We've specialized ourselves into a very limited field. We've been out of the mainstream a long time and a lot has happened. . . while we sit hoping that it will all go away.

The answer, I believe, is to get back to

"art directing and everything."

We have to realize that Design *is*, Photography *is*, Illustration *was* — unless we recognize all the methods of illustration.

To me, illustration is only a sometime part of visual communication. Illustration can be fine art, and fine art can be illustration. Illustration can be typography. Illustration can be photography. It can be almost anything. . . executed by almost anyone.

We do not live dangerously in our work, but are too preoccupied with the security of the hand-painted picture as illustration. I'm fortunate I guess and am not hurt when someone fails to call me an illustrator. This word "illustrator" has never had much glory in my part of the country because no one has ever known what an illustrator was. Saying "I am an illustrator" is like saying "God is dead" to an atheist.

Therefore, like the church, we have a semantic problem and have to study our symbols and see if they still mean the same thing they used to mean, to Man, right now!

We've got to integrate. We've got to admit that there are other forms of illustration. I've never seen such a segregated bunch of people as we are. When will we present in our shows the best in illustration — whether it be photography, painting, drawing, design, or some other graphic medium?

I'm afraid that if an aware, alert individual should appear at this address, at any time or at the very moment we think we are at our best, he would go away thinking that our only purpose was the celebration of graphite and pigment.

Now is the time for us to cease being amazed by ourselves; to become sensitive to all things and react to all things, and to express this unique, individual reaction in our unique way.

Each of us is unique. No matter who we are, if we are breathing we are unique, and it is our responsibility to be ourselves and express this uniqueness. Only we can do this, no other soul can do this for us. The other soul might help us or open the way, but we have to do it for ourselves. Be certain that what you have to offer is *you* and not some imitation of someone else, because he has already given his or has it to give.

Give *yours* in *your* name.

As a final note: Please remember that while I'm talking to you, I am screaming at myself. ▪

Art: In Churches, In the Kitchen
by Charles Schorre
Ramparts Magazine,
Vol. 5, No. 2, July 1966

Thoughts: If I have to go back into history to have my religious experience, I cannot have one. Someone else, living in that time in history, has already had it for me. An historical event, if misused in this manner, is adult thumb-sucking. It is an excuse for the individual to bypass his own religious experience, a symbol of his noninvolvement. If this historical religious experience is his *only* experience, he can't be blamed if something goes wrong; he can't be blamed if someone "proves" it didn't happen; he can't be blamed for not having the guts or courage to have his own religious experience. He's afraid it might be the wrong thing to do; it might be "out" or "camp"; it might be the wrong thing to do that year, just as Christ's being on the cross was the wrong thing to do that year.

Some of these things became a reality to me while working (since early 1950) on a theme of crucifixion-birth. . . life-death. . . to die to become. . . stop, turn around, go again, live again. . . in another direction.

At first I just *had* to witness a hospital birth. I *had* to tie a cadaver (as near Christ's physical appearance as I could find) to a cross. I *had* to get a live man and rope him to the same cross. Some of these things could not be realized at the time: "Staph disease" in hospitals, couldn't get a doctor or hospital staff to let me in. I wanted to go to Mexico or some place and "be there" when a woman delivered her own baby rather primitively. This wasn't realized either.

Then it dawned on me that if all these things could be accomplished, the end result, no matter how successful, would still only be an *illustration* of an historical event —"They could have used a brighter color in the stained glass around the head of Christ"— the way all critics aren't involved. Unless you are in it, working with it, doing it, building it, with your hands and mind and feet and anything else that's handy. Like being a large file cabinet, full of facts about love, an authority, yet never having been there just once. A living dead authority; go to the Holy Land and see where *they* did it. I started to realize that I might use some facts, historical facts as a crutch, or springboard, but if anything authentic was going to happen it was going to have to come from me.

Recently about 14 "religious paintings" were on exhibit in the Chapel (Rice University campus). Because they were "religious paintings," no "art authority" committed himself in print about the exhibit. It was stimulating, however, to find the great number of people who weren't particularly educated about art who accepted a JFK assassination painting, a heart painting, a love painting, a birth painting, and a landscape in a "religious art" show.

The movies *Patch of Blue* and *Zorba the Greek* were religious experiences for me; I have also had them in churches, in the kitchen washing the dishes with my wife, with my children in the backyard, with persons in strange places, with a life class in a university.

Are we "saved"? It is up to each one of us to live up to our salvation with all we have in us, to be with all of our being. If we don't, we are slobs, slopping through life, no matter how clever, beautiful, rich, lucky, talented, charitable, or religious. ▪

Charles Schorre and his colors
by Patricia C. Johnson
Houston Chronicle, November 18, 1981

Charles Schorre is not getting older, he's getting better. The series of recent paintings on display at DuBose Gallery reflect this artist's continuous exploration of emotions as revealed through color or gesture.

Although Schorre does not work sequentially — he works on several different paintings at one time and alternates between photography, painting and drawing — there are four distinct "types" of paintings in the show: the glove or hand image; the abstractions of pure and intense color; a group of small and sedate paintings reminiscent of his photography/collage series, *Pages From Books Unpublished*; and a series of "landscapes."

The distinction, however, refers to a superficial image because what the paintings deal with is surface textures, the emotive properties of colors and an intuitive approach to painting. Not all the paintings are successful; some, in fact, are no more than happy accidents of decoration. But when Schorre is at his best, he is masterful.

In the large and vibrant canvases like *God'sign*, a violet and emerald hand shape, suspended in yellow background, or *Nocturnal Godsong*, a rich beige sand and black painting that encompasses the violet end of the spectrum, Schorre variously screams and whispers of an inner spirit. In some, color alone is not enough and an energized line emerges as lightning out of the skies.

One particularly beautiful "landscape" is entitled *Canyon de Chellyellow*. Rather than describing the canyon in terms of natural beauty, Schorre uses his expert technique to create an illusion of the peace and wonder such settings elicit. Acrylic washes are applied as if they were watercolor to form transparent layers of color. The sky-ground relationship is ambiguous, diffused by the shimmering quality of the canyon's facade, then electrically unified by a dramatic gesture, a streak of lightning.

But the most poetic of the works are the monotone paintings. Generally smaller in scale, paintings like *God'scream* and *Godance* have no activity, no subject. Rather, they are elusive spaces made of veils of color that recede and emerge to form fields of energy. In *God'scream* a pastel-shade curtain with a torn center of white — one of the rare paintings in which a brushstroke is visible — reveals not the void left by what must be so terrifying a sound, but rather its emotionally charged echo. ■

Charles Schorre: Painter-Illustrator of Houston
by Norman Kent
American Artist, September 1961

Many readers will recall the fine figure drawing by Charles Schorre reproduced on the cover of our November 1960 issue and the promise made then that we would present him later in a feature article. We had an opportunity to renew our acquaintance with him when he visited New York this spring and, out of a large body of work he had brought from Houston, to select the pieces reproduced in this article.

From what I observed in Houston two years ago, the climate for art there is a challenging one. Her artists and illustrators are fired with purpose; their output, like everything else in Texas, is enormous. A building boom is making Houston one of the fastest growing cities in the Southwest, bringing in new business and residents.

In this period of spectacular civic growth, the artists of Houston might be expected to allow their prodigious energies to serve industry without much regard for creative qualities, to reap a whirlwind, and to be satisfied with an ordinary performance as long as the client pays the bill. Happily, this is not

the case. Seldom have I witnessed such genuine concern to meet national standards, as evidenced by the fine work of the Artists Guild of Houston show which I helped to jury in 1959. This opinion is reinforced by Len Leone, art director of Bantam Books, who has recently returned from serving as one of this year's jurors.

Sometimes the New York tag subjects an artist-juror to an uncomfortable patronage or to a feeling of resentment on the part of local artists — especially after the jury work is done, the formality of first meeting is over, and the socializing begins. But not in Houston. There a visiting artist is regarded as a fellow craftsman; no pedestal is provided, and he is not expected to be an oracle. As a result, conversation for him among a group of Houston artists is an easy give and take.

Competition among Houston artists is keen, but pride in the special accomplishments of a few outstanding talents permeates the whole group. While most of the work I saw there represented commissions executed for advertising agencies and printers, two special accents characterized the best examples. The first of these was the fresh contemporary spirit of layout, typography and illustration; the second the strong draughtsmanship that indicated good disciplined training and constant independent practice. On inquiry I found that many of these illustrators and designers were active painters outside of their commercial assignments. Several Houston dealers in fine arts represent a number of them, and sales of the work of Texas painters in general — affected by the cultural atmosphere of two universities (Rice and Houston), two art museums, and a celebrated symphony — are on the increase. Schorre, however, prefers to sell his paintings and drawings from his own studio. As a watercolorist he is proud of his recent (1961) election to the American Watercolor Society, following several years of representation in its annual exhibitions.

Charles Schorre would be outstanding in any artistic community, but in Houston he occupies a special position, due in large measure to his success in two camps. His work as an illustrator is charged with those independent qualities we usually associate with the realm of painting, whereas his production as a draughtsman and painter is in nowise colored by his long practice as a commissioned artist. This ability to create a strong identity in both departments without succumbing to the pitfalls of expediency requires a disciplined mind. Self-analysis constantly applied lies back of the Schorre determination. It is revealed in the following statements:

"My methods of working are about as varied as my taste in music. I look upon style or school or any other classification as a handicap. Style to me is another brush or another color. Working with only one size tool would definitely help to develop an immediate style, but it would also restrict one to a limited viewpoint. Art to me is the experience of producing, and I can only gain that by painting in different manners. If an artist forgets about style, his viewpoint can be unlimited. Some artists paint only in one fashion, whereas I work in as many ways as I feel capable. In my teaching I encourage this point of view, for it challenges one to grow both technically and artistically. Holding to one manner or even to one medium is too limiting, and I feel strongly that constant experimentation enables us to experience more as artists.

"My concern for communication is primary. I feel that our present obsession with being different is at times a great sickness. . . conception and communication seldom get the consideration they deserve. We seem to be concerned with the body of the car rather than its engine. If there is no concept, the labor that follows is fruitless, as far as I am concerned.

"I usually work on as many as six jobs in various media at one time, some commissioned and others independent of contract. Whenever my excitement for one dulls, I stop work and turn to another. This means that I probably produce less than other artists, but I am fortunate in having clients who permit me abundant time to complete particular jobs; to insure this working method, I must necessarily turn down work with short deadlines."

Like most artists, Schorre did not come to these conclusions overnight, nor was his philosophy developed without a lot of independent thinking about life and art. In my long conversation with him I sensed his deep love of humanity and his real humility. These characteristics shine through his work, especially in his independent drawings and paintings — like the long project he undertook this past year in a personal reaction to the awesome Crucifixion, which he told me had caused him many hours of anguish and frustration until, after many trials, he evolved a solution.

Born in Cuero, Texas, in 1925, Charles Schorre was graduated from the University of Texas in 1948 with a Bachelor of Fine Arts degree in sculpture and painting. After working in the bull pen of a Houston advertising agency for two years, where he learned the basic techniques of commercial procedure, he became an art director of

Foote, Cone and Belding for the next four years. Since 1954 he has been a free-lance illustrator, except for some part-time teaching at the Museum of Fine Arts — first for a year of night classes in 1948, and then in 1958 teaching a day class in advanced life painting and drawing, followed this past spring with another special class in portrait painting.

About two years ago Schorre and five other free-lance artists moved into an unusual studio building on the outskirts of Houston. Conceived by Jim Glass, the single-story structure was designed by David D. Red of the architectural department of the University of Houston, and its landscaping was planned by Robert F. White. Modern in style, the L-shaped, low lying building consists of five private studios on its north side, each of which has a door opening onto a forty by sixty-foot patio. An office for a secretary-receptionist, a conference room, and a fully-equipped photographic studio and darkroom complete the ideally arranged room sections.

Schorre occupies the largest of the private studios (seventeen by eighteen feet). All of the windows on the north side, on a wall canted about fifteen percent from bottom to top and overhung by a roof projection, provide perfect natural light. Each studio has interior walls of pine, with built-in cabinets, exposed beam ceilings, and of course, each is completely air-conditioned. A pool and fountain in the patio, with two large parking areas adjoining, complete this ideal installation.

In this atmosphere of peace and utility Charles Schorre spends his working days. For the concentration he feels so essential to his art, all Schorre has to do is shut his studio door and he is in a world apart; when he wants company or criticism his associates are nearby. Each, he told me, respects the other fellow's privacy, but as a group there is a fine spirit of fraternity and frequent collaboration.

I have touched briefly on Schorre's general philosophy, but his technical variety also needs some coverage. Having worked as an art director, and today often retained as a consultant in this exacting field, he long ago learned to make comprehensive sketches of a complete idea. First he thoroughly familiarizes himself with the problem involved and then, with a series of rough graphic sketches, visualizes the format of the whole advertisement so that the illustration, however dominant it might finally be, will be

B. Franklin *ND. Ink and acrylic on illustration board, 13¾ x 6½ inches. Artist's Collection. Illustration for Brown & Root Construction Company, D'Arcy Advertising Agency.*
(Shown in original article.)

integrated into the whole concept. Never satisfied with a single arrangement, Schorre habitually makes many roughs for each job, but submits a single comprehensive sketch to his client. In explanation he says: "I do not recommend the several solutions idea for those who want to avoid frustration, but for me the making of multiple choices is the only way I can work and feel that I am an artist of some creative ability.

"I enjoy working in this part of the country because we have fewer specialists than in New York or on the West Coast. Consequently, I think of an advertisement or whatever commission I am working on in its entirety. I feel that this obligation of conceiving the whole plan allows me more free-

dom to do a better job than if, as illustrator or painter only, I were called in to execute the pictorial element only."

Since Schorre arbitrarily divides his time equally between commissioned work and his easel pictures, there is often only a fine line of demarcation between the two. He writes: "I am fortunate that my hours of work and a great part of my hours of pleasure are devoted to the same thing. Having an understanding wife and family helps to make this possible. Ninety percent of my advertising illustration ends up framed on office (clients') walls, but first it has to perform a job of merchandising for the purchaser. It should be firmly stated that I do not think of this aspect of my work in terms of gallery pictures, but at the same time I do try to get as much painting quality into them as I do in my independent pictures."

About three quarters of Schorre's work in advertising illustration dramatizes heavy industry — oil and oil machinery. And since much of it has a natural outdoor setting, it is little wonder that this artist has found as much romance in oil derricks as certain Dutch painters found in windmills.

As an inveterate experimenter in media and technique, Schorre draws constantly on a study of the masters, as well as deriving benefit from the work of his contemporaries. While he disclaims a preference or a practice of any one style, it is my opinion that the emotional overtones in his painting align him with the *essence* of abstract composition without a loss of recognizable form. This character is illustrated in the color plate reproduced in this article, and to a marked degree in the giant pressroom scene in which Schorre has capitalized on the radiating lines to produce an electrically charged atmosphere. Incidentally, Schorre told me that this job fell to him because photographic attempts failed to produce the qualities the client wished to see dramatized. This is certainly a proof that photographic realism does not always fill the bill.

In concluding this report on Charles Schorre, one final aspect of his work, and one that underlies all he does, deserves special commendation. That is his creative draughtsmanship. He draws constantly, and it is this basic foundation that gives all his painting its personal flavor, its freedom from prosaic tightness that always seems to stop short of one more stroke. If only more painters made more drawings... ∎

Charles Schorre:
Artist's Handbook
by Dave Crossley
SPOT, Summer 1985

Charles Schorre's resumé has near the beginning the words "Considers himself reclusive. . . lives and works in Houston, Texas." Is he saying that he's reclusive because he lives and works there? Or that he lives and works there because he's reclusive? Or, if asked, would he say, as he so often does, "I don't know, I never thought about that before."

Schorre defines himself as a painter and insists he is not a very good photographer. He also insists that he's a hermit, that he's old (he's 60), that he's still a child, and that he really doesn't know what he's doing until he's done it. He uses photography extensively in his paintings, affixing his photographs to the surface of the work where it seems they were always meant to be. The process he uses requires some serendipity: paintings are painted and photographs are photographed and later, while looking at a painting he'll remember a photograph that is stored away somewhere in his studio (which should be a national treasure and open to the public) and soon he's leaning over the work carefully positioning the print, which now looks, miraculously, as though it had been made precisely to fit in that place on that painting.

Schorre calls his manner of working intuitive. He goes into the studio each day without a plan and begins to paint and to scrabble around and observe as things begin to come together. He always has five or six projects going on at the same time. When one fails of solution he moves to another "station" in the studio. He loves scratches and marks, fossils and shapes, and he notes them everywhere, then gives himself over to his memory while he works.

One of his memories is of time he spent as a designer in advertising. He did a lot of photography then and learned how to make work that was simple and communicated fast. That experience has left him with a love of printing and publishing. In conjunction with his painting, he has steadily worked on two series since 1969: *Artist's Handbook* (selections of which are published here) and *Pages From Books Unpublished*, some of which have used pictures from the handbook. He is now working with Houston designer Jerry Herring to publish the *Artist's Handbook.*

What follows is his side of a conversation about the *Artist's Handbook:*

———

"I started out photographing people who use their hands to make their livelihood and then I focused just on artists and then I returned to everyman, realizing that there were a lot of people I wanted to photograph who didn't call themselves artists. Basically, *Artist's Handbook* is a silent, visual answer to the question, How do you do it? It started out as a polemic against how to paint or how to photograph or how to do anything books. I never taught technique or anything like that because if you came to me to learn how to do it and in a year you learned, it would take you ten years to forget about it. All that time you're standing in the wing waiting to come on stage and by the time you come on you're all dried up, gone. I'm against all how to do it. You have to learn, but as soon as that's over, you have to forget it.

"Once I was asked by a publisher to do a how to paint book, and the more I got into it I realized I didn't believe what I was attempting to do; it was a sacrilegious brainwash. That's when I realized that my how to book, the *Artist's Handbook* would have no words except their signatures and their birth dates and maybe a foreword or afterword.

"Another realization came to me with the *Pages From Books Unpublished* series. I like to make books but at that time — fifteen years ago — there seemed to be no publishers in this part of the country. I was frustrated and the answer to this frustration became a series of unpublished spreads that are now a big part of my art. The spread is the art. The pages inform my paintings and the paintings inform the pages.

"The first *Artist's Handbook* photographs were part of the first *Pages*. The first complete hand thing had two 8 x 10 images, one of Aaron Siskind and one of Gyorgy Kepes, and about 60 face/palm pictures that were contact prints with written notations to me about their future use. It was a sort of notebook of process, to myself.

"I have pictures of approximately 50-60 painters and sculptors, 10 writers, 12 graphic designers, 20 photographers. Over 100 in all. It's getting to be a problem because I'm trying to get model releases from everybody now and some people aren't cooperating and some are dead and their estates aren't

cooperating. A guy like Robert Motherwell, whom I didn't get one from at the time, is now so cloistered and surrounded by people that I can't get to him. He's seen the little booklet I've printed and he likes it but he lost it, and then when I sent a model release people were afraid to get him to sign it. I just can't get to him. I don't know his phone number, it's unlisted. After a day and a half of trying I realized I had to start painting, I was tired of this stuff. When it becomes a hassle I stop.

"I like to boil things down to their essential elements, like the silhouette of a hand.

George Krause

What I need is the man or woman's face and their hands. That's all I want. I first ask them to do a certain thing; hold your hands up by your ears, palms facing me. I shoot that and then I say 'Do you want to vary that in any way?' and sometimes when they get into these variations it's very interesting.

"Usually, I use the controlled picture, but if a variation is so important I use it in juxtaposition with the control, and sometimes eliminate the control entirely. When I shot Barbara Rose, for her variation she chose almost a judo stance, and I like it better than the control, because that's almost the way she was when she was here at the Museum of Fine Arts.

"I don't worry about the background. I've stripped it down and if the background interferes, that's a problem. I want to get a sort of a straight mug shot, police lineup thing. It's just a common photograph, so the only thing of real interest there intellectually or artistically would be this face and these hands. I'm not really interested in the connection with the background, but when it happens, as in the Witkin picture, that is very interesting.

"These photographs are antidesign. I like to design, so I decided to boil these things down and not have any design, boil it down to what I want. I don't want that guy to comb his hair. I don't want that girl to put her dress on in a certain way. I'm not going to just shoot her in her bedroom. I want it to just happen to be.

"On the surface, the thing I'm asking people to do for these pictures is silly. Some sophisticated people don't care to do it. There was one German photographer who first rejected the idea, then begged me to

Robert Mapplethorpe

shoot him after he realized that I had photographed several of his gods. I shot him to make him feel good, but I shot him out of focus, which is not at all hard for me to do, but I did that on purpose.

"When you ask some people it's almost as if you said 'Take your clothes off for a minute.' People like Jim Dine and Lee Friedlander — who are friends and both rejected me at different times although they didn't know it. Lee spent about three hours coming over here and visiting and talking and finally I said 'You're here to tell me you don't want to do it, aren't you?' and he said yeah. It's odd, because he's a sort of invader of privacy too. I had a violent argument with Garry Winogrand, but he finally wanted me to do it. I said it didn't matter to me, and as soon as I said that, it was his turn, and he agreed. It's like a bullfight sometimes.

"Sometimes they backfire. I was at a conference and ran into former Governor Jerry Brown of California and I showed him my little booklet and asked if he would let me photograph him in that manner. Well, all that time I should have known he wasn't lis-

tening, he was looking over my shoulder. But he said 'Yeah, I'll do it, but we have to hurry, where do you want me?' I said 'Just stand there and put your hands up by your ears' and he said 'I'm not going to do that' so I said 'Well, forget it, that's okay, go about your business.' He's like the German: if he finally caught on to what I was doing, he might be interested in it, but I don't have time to fool around. I have to do it fast, I have to explain fast what I'm doing.

"I approached William Wegman the night of his opening at Texas Gallery in Houston and he asked me 'What are you doing this for? How did you start?' I told him and I thought he was listening but he wasn't. The next morning when I came to shoot him he asked the same questions that he asked me the night before. It's not very hard to catch on to. I'm not going to dress the dog up and have him eat cake or anything. But a lot of people have such a hard time getting into it it's pitiful. Some people get it fast. Some people think it's a riot. Some people are just suspicious.

"Sometimes I scare the hell out of them. I dominate them and scare them off. I can identify the ego immediately. As soon as I explain the thing, that's one of the things that comes out. The ego is identified fast. It's revealed. If it's someone who's on stage all the time, someone who thinks he's the greatest artist, it comes out real fast. That might be why some of them are really embarrassed; the greatest artist in his own mind might have a hard time doing this humbling thing. It's not a normal position to put your hands in.

"The hands are very important. Robert Motherwell, when he walked out of the room after I shot his photograph, mumbled something and I said 'What did you say?' and he said 'My hands are so small.' I said 'What difference does that make?' And he said 'They're so small, for what I do.' Things like that are really interesting.

"Sometimes the hands play almost as big a part as the face. It's a real identification tag, and I haven't even thought about what a palmist might say.

"Sometimes I'll go to hear someone speak and not take my camera because I don't shoot photographs at night, so I'm hampered by my manner, my technique. When it becomes any kind of a hassle, I don't do it.

I do it mostly with grace when people come by the studio. I can just say, 'Let's go outside and shoot your photograph.'

"Once when I had a show in New York, I walked out of the gallery just to get away for a moment and I saw a policeman there with white gloves on. I asked him to do it, but to leave his gloves on and he held his hands a little away from his head and I backed him up against the building right next to Parke Bernet. I didn't realize how intense I was being and I was back by the garbage can and people were walking around us because they thought I was holding him up with a camera gun of some sort. It was weird, and I didn't know it until after it was over.

"They actually stood around kind of watching, waiting for something to go off. No one touched me. A guy told me he couldn't figure out how I was holding this cop up with a camera.

"It's such an antithesis of the way I go about things. I work in an intuitive manner as an artist, and then when I'm working on this series as a photographer, I ask them to do this particular thing, the same thing of everyone, and so that's a control thing, which leaves me on a kind of a see-saw.

"I don't want to get too far into photography because I'm really not a photographer. But I always heralded photography as art before people in this town even saw the *Family of Man* show.

"There's lots of things I've tried to do for photography and I still do. But now it's a contagious disease, it's almost gotten out of hand. But I still use it in my work and it informs my paintings.

"It's a way of note-taking that I consider very valuable.

"It's fun to do it when I feel like it. I'm not stalking people, so I miss a lot of people I really want and perhaps will never see again, but I'm not in the mood that day or I'm without a camera or film. Since I'm a painter, I fail to realize that being ready is part of it. It can be joyful, meeting people for only a few seconds that I would not otherwise meet, since I'm not a very social person. I have a good time when I go to a party, but it's hard for me to get there. This project is an excuse for me to say hello to someone for an intense minute. It's amazing what people say and do in these moments.

"It appears to be foolish but I don't look upon this endeavor as foolish. I sometimes feel it is the essence of the person I photograph and this always gives me a feeling of deep respect for the human being and what he or she is doing. It's an intense experience and one that I appreciate very much. I'll probably do it as long as I live." ∎

Charles Schorre was born in Cuero, Texas, in 1925. In 1948, he graduated from the University of Texas–Austin with a BFA, then married Margaret Storm and set up residence in Houston. He and his wife had three daughters and eight grandchildren. Schorre taught classes and led workshops at the Museum of Fine Arts, Houston (1949-50), and Rice University (1960-72). Later, in 1974 he conducted a month-long university workshop in Guadalajara, Mexico, and in 1978 he led an outdoor figure drawing workshop in Ingram, Texas. In 1963, Schorre began traveling throughout the United States observing mental health facilities in preparation for designing, illustrating, and partially editing *Planning, Programming, and Design for the Community Mental Health Center* (1965) for which he won a number of awards. He went on in 1968 to design, edit, and partially illustrate *Life Class*, listed among the Fifty Best Books of the Year by the American Institute of Graphic Arts. Schorre would receive awards from the International Typographic Society and the Watercolor Society only to sever, as a protest, all connections with professional organizations in 1970. After starting his *Emerge* series in 1956, he initiated the *Artist's Handbook* series in 1970, and by 1971 he had embarked on his extensive *Pages From Books Unpublished* series. In 1977, the same year he was awarded a poster commission from the American Academy in Rome, he began his *Art Lessons* series. In 1979, Mobil Corporation awarded Schorre an Artist-in-Residence grant for a stay in Saudi Arabia. He also received that year a National Endowment for the Arts grant. He would later attend the 34th International Design Conference in Aspen, Colorado, as a National Endowment Fellow. Schorre was named Texas Artist of the Year in 1986 and received the City of Houston Mayor's Award for Outstanding Contribution to the Arts. He would subsequently be selected to participate in a group exhibition for the 1990 Economic Summit of Industrialized Nations held at Rice University. In 1993, he received the Educator Award from the American Institute of Architecture. In July 1996, Schorre died in Houston.

Group Exhibitions

1946   *Permanent U.S. Marine Corps Exhibition* Washington, D.C.

1947   *Texas Fine Arts Association Statewide Circuit Exhibition*

The Ninth Texas General Exhibition, Dallas

Caller-Times National Exhibition, Corpus Christi, Texas

1948   *First Central States Graphic Arts Annual,* Joslyn Memorial Art Museum, Omaha, Nebraska

First Southwestern Print Annual, Dallas Museum of Art, Dallas

1949   *Eleventh Annual Texas Exhibition of Painting and Sculpture,* Witte Memorial Museum, San Antonio

1965   *Houston Annual Area Exhibition,* Houston; received first award in painting

1966   *Houston Exhibition '66,* Houston; received first award

1969   *First Southwestern States Watercolor Annual;* received first award

1970   *103rd Annual/American Watercolor Society,* New York; received Windsor Newton Award

1971   *Fourteenth Annual Delta Art Exhibition,* The Arkansas Arts Center; Brian O'Doherty, juror

1972   *Artists Against the War,* New York; traveling exhibition

1973   *Private Works,* Contemporary Arts Museum, Houston

1975   *Artists Make Toys,* Art Museum of South Texas, Corpus Christi, Texas

20th Exhibition of Southwestern Prints and Drawings, Museum of Fine Arts, Dallas

1976   *Houston Area Annual,* Houston; received first award

1977   *Conversations with Artists,* University of Houston, Clear Lake City, Texas

Portraits: the Mental Picture, AIGA Galleries, New York; traveling exhibition

Cronin Gallery, Houston

International Drawing Biennale, United Kingdom

1978   *Prints from Little Egypt Enterprises,* Moody Gallery, Houston

Works on Paper/Southwest, Museum of Fine Arts, Dallas

1979   *American Drawings II,* Virginia Museum of Art, Portsmouth

51 Drawings, Smithsonian Institution, Washington, D.C.; traveling exhibition

Works on Paper, Nave Museum, Victoria, Texas

Doors, Alley Theatre, Houston

Miniature Show, Lawndale Annex, University of Houston, Houston

Pictures in Picture Magazine, Cityscape Photo Gallery, Los Angeles

Some Houston Photographers, Museum of Fine Arts School, Houston

1980   *Houston Area Exhibition,* Sarah Campbell Blaffer Gallery, University of Houston, Houston; William C. Agee, Linda Cathcart, Harris Rosenstein, jurors

1980 New Orleans Triennial, New Orleans Museum of Art, New Orleans; Marcia Tucker, juror

1981   *Invitational '81,* Longview Museum & Arts Center, Longview, Texas

Impressions of Houston, O'Kane Gallery, University of Houston, Houston

Masks, Little Egypt Enterprises, Houston

1982   *Flowers & Gardens in American Painting,* DuBose Gallery, Houston

Texas on Paper, Contemporary Arts Museum, Houston; circulated by Independent Curators, Inc., New York

The Americans: The Collage, Contemporary Arts Museum, Houston; catalogue

Art from Houston in Norway: 1982; catalogue

Selected Prints From Little Egypt Enterprises, Harris Gallery, Houston

Recent Purchases, Museum of Fine Arts, Houston

Color, DuBose Gallery, Houston

Premier Event Group Show, Mid-Town Art Center, Houston

1983   *A Salute to Houston Artists,* Mid-Town Art Center, Houston

Contemporary Photoworks II, Albuquerque, New Mexico

The Contemporaries, Glassell School of Art, Museum of Fine Arts, Houston

Suzanne Paul, Charles Schorre, K.C. Williams, Texas Gallery, Houston

1984   *Artists Call Against U.S. Intervention in Central America,* SoHo Gallery, Austin, Texas

The Houston School. . . Fresh Roots/First Marks, The Drawing Room Gallery, Houston

AIGA Graphic Design USA 5, The American Institute of Graphic Arts Gallery, New York

Public Art, DiverseWorks, Houston

1984 Show, Houston Center, Houston

Assistance League-84, Hyatt Regency, Houston; Peter Marzio, judge

Texas Visions, Transco Tower Gallery, Houston

Houston Drawing Show, Glassell School of Art, Museum of Fine Arts, Houston

1985   *The Houston School. . . Fresh Roots/First Marks,* The Drawing Room Gallery, Houston

The New Nude, Mid-Town Art Center, Houston; catalogue

Fresh Paint, Museum of Fine Arts, Houston; catalogue

Expose: Fourth Annual Members' Exhibition, Houston Center for Photography, Houston

Layering, an Art of Time & Space, The Albuquerque Museum, Albuquerque, New Mexico; catalogue

The Avant Old Guard, Cullen Center, Houston

1986   *Posters*, Goethe Institute, Houston

Eight Artists–Houston–Aspen, Patricia Moore Gallery, Aspen, Colorado

Houston International Photofest, Houston

The Texas Landscape, 1900–1986, Museum of Fine Arts, Houston; catalogue

American Landscape, 1870-1986, Meredith Long & Company, Houston

Texas Visions, Transco Tower Gallery, Houston; catalogue

Prisoners of Conscience, DiverseWorks, Houston

Artists Choose Artists, Art League of Houston, Houston

Texas Annual 1986, Texas Fine Art Association, Laguna Gloria Art Museum, Austin, Texas; Walter Hopps, curator; catalogue

Plates by Houston Painters, Perception Galleries, Houston

The Photographic Print: Extending the Limits, Houston Center for Photography, Houston

1987   *From the Object: Still Life Themes & Variations*, Glassell School of Art, Museum of Fine Arts, Houston; catalogue

Houston Photographers, Northlight Gallery, Arizona State University, Tempe, Arizona

Selections, 15 Years, Little Egypt Enterprises, Art League of Houston, Houston

Photo-Technology: An Exploration of the Electronic Imaging Environment, Houston Center for Photography, Houston

The Anatomy of Drawing, Hooks-Epstein Galleries, Inc., Houston

Toy Show, Victoria Regional Museum, Victoria, Texas; Dianne David, curator

Abstract Sensibilities Now, Lawndale Art & Performance Center, Houston; Sally Sprout, curator

One Eye, Houston Center for Photography, Houston; Jack Massing, curator

Third Coast Review: A Look at Art in Texas, Aspen Art Museum, Aspen, Colorado; Annette D. Carlozzi, curator

1988   *Houston 88*, Cullen Center, Houston; Marti Mayo, Neil Printz, Anne Tucker, Marilyn Zeitlin, jurors

Houston International Fotofest, Houston; catalogue

Praise God! Little Egypt Enterprises, Houston

1988 Houston Area Exhibition, Sarah Campbell Blaffer Gallery, University of Houston, Houston; Allison de Lima Green, Edward and Nancy Kienholz, Richard Koshalek, jurors

Mask Show, Little Egypt Enterprises, Houston

1989   *Toy Show*, Transco Tower Gallery, Houston, and Amarillo Art Center, Amarillo, Texas

Texas Accountants and Lawyers for the Arts, Houston

Intimate Collages, The Watson Gallery, Houston

Beyond Permission, Houston Center for Photography, Houston; catalogue

Another Reality, Hooks-Epstein Gallery, Houston

Important Works on Paper, Meredith Long & Company, Houston

Masters' Choice, Art League of Houston, Houston

Messages from the South, Sewall Art Gallery, Rice University, Houston

1990   *Field and Forest / American Landscapes*, Meredith Long & Company, Houston

Printmaking in Texas–The 1980's, Modern Art Museum of Fort Worth, Fort Worth, Texas; catalogue

The Figure in the 20th Century, Meredith Long & Company, Houston

Tradition and Innovation: A Museum Celebration of Texas Art, Museum of Fine Arts, Houston

Texas Artists: Another Reality, McNay Museum, San Antonio

Organic Abstractions, Rudder Exhibit Hall, Texas A&M University, College Station, Texas

1991   *Shadow Images*, Hooks-Epstein Gallery, Houston

Important Works on Paper, Meredith Long & Company, Houston

Island Inspired, Transco Tower Gallery, Houston

1992   *Other Ways*, North Harris College Gallery, Houston

1993   *Personal Attachments*, Hooks-Epstein Gallery, Houston

Artist's Progress, Seven Houston Artists 1943-1993, Glassell School of Art, Museum of Fine Arts, Houston

Little Egypt Enterprises, 1974-1993, DiverseWorks, Houston

1994   *Landscape Without Figures*, Hooks-Epstein Gallery, Houston

Miniatures, Hooks-Epstein Gallery, Houston

1995   *Tri Delta Show for Charity*, Houston Engineering Society Building, Houston

Solo Exhibitions

1964   *Charles Schorre: Cruciforms*, Rice University, Houston

1965   *Charles Schorre*, University of Texas Art Museum, Austin, Texas

1966   *Charles Schorre*, DuBose Gallery, Houston

1968   *Charles Schorre*, DuBose Gallery, Houston

1969   *Charles Schorre/Photographs*, Latent Image Gallery, Houston

1970   *Charles Schorre*, DuBose Gallery, Houston

1974   *Drawings, Collages & Paintings*, Laguna Gloria Art Museum, Austin, Texas

       Charles Schorre/ A Retrospective, DuBose Gallery, Houston

1976   *Charles Schorre*, DuBose Gallery, Houston

1977   *Charles Schorre*, DuBose Gallery, Houston

       Charles Schorre/Retrospective, Historical Museum, Cuero, Texas

1978   *Charles Schorre*, David B. Findlay Gallery, New York

       Charles Schorre: Recent Works, Texas A&M University, College Station, Texas

1979   *Visions from Saudi Arabia, France, Ireland and the Texas Hill Country*, DuBose Gallery, Houston

1980   *Charles Schorre*, Wildine Galleries, Albuquerque, New Mexico

       Charles Schorre/Retrospective, Nave Museum, Victoria, Texas

1981   *Charles Schorre: Pages From Books Unpublished*, CEPA Gallery, Buffalo, New York, and Contemporary Arts Museum, Houston

       Charles Schorre, DuBose Gallery, Houston

1982   *Charles Schorre*, Texas Gallery, Houston

1983   *Charles Schorre: Paintings and Drawings*, DuBose Gallery, Houston

1984   *Charles Schorre: Pages From Books Unpublished*, Film in the Cities Gallery, St. Paul, Minnesota

       Canvas and Paperworks– Charles Schorre, Meredith Long & Company, Houston

1985   *Charles Schorre*, Joan Hodgell Gallery, Sarasota, Florida

1986   *Paintings & Collages*, Meredith Long & Company, Houston

1988   *Photocollages*, Meredith Long & Company, Houston

1989   *Charles Schorre*, Meredith Long & Company, Houston

       Charles Schorre: Photocollages, MSC Forsyth Center Galleries, Texas A&M University, College Station, Texas; catalogue

1990   *Charles Schorre*, Jung Center, Houston

1991   *Charles Schorre*, Meredith Long & Company, Houston

1992   *Charles Schorre Photo Collages*, Meredith Long & Company, Houston

1995   *Charles Schorre–Recent Paintings*, Meredith Long & Company, Houston

Selected Public Collections

American Artists Group, New York

American Bank, Houston

Baylor College of Medicine, Houston

Citicorp, Inc., New York

Corum Energy, Houston

Cowles Communications

CRM Publications

Crown Zellerbach

ESSO Eastern

Exxon, New York

Exxon USA

First Bank of Minneapolis, Minnesota

Hallmark, Inc.

Hooker Chemical, Houston

Hyatt Regency

Insurance Corporation of America, Houston

Interfin Corporation, Houston

Lifemark, Houston

Mobil Corporation

Museum of Fine Arts, Houston

National Endowment for the Arts

National Football League

Neiman-Marcus, Dallas

Oxirane Corporation, Houston

Playboy

Psychology Today

Revere Petroleum, Houston

St. Luke's Episcopal Hospital, Houston

Schlumberger

Sheldon Memorial Art Gallery, University of Nebraska, Lincoln

Shell Oil Corporation

Southwest Gulf Petroleum, Houston

Teledyne Exploration

Texas Commerce Bank, Houston

Texas Eastern Transmission, Houston

Texas Energy, Houston

Transco, Houston

Transworld Airways, Kansas City

United Gas, Houston

U.S. Marine Corps

Westchase Hilton Hotel, Houston

Wilson Industries, Houston

Zapata Corporation, Houston

Modern Art Museum of Fort Worth, Fort Worth, Texas

Bibliography

1957 Downes, Bruce. "The Nude in Photography – Is it Art?" *Popular Photography Color Annual,* 1957.

1958 Geeslin, Campbell. "Museum's School Adds Scope." *The Houston Post,* August 1958.

1961 Kent, Norman. "Painter-illustrator of Houston." *American Artist,* September 1961.

1963 Swinkels, Gilles (Mark St. Gill). "An Illustrator Talks About Art." *Houston Chronicle,* June 9, 1963.

Kent, Norman. "A Portfolio of Drawings by Charles Schorre." *American Artist,* November 1963.

1965 "Charles Schorre's Art Work Featured." *The Daily Texan,* March 28, 1965.

White, Ralph. *Charles Schorre.* Exh. cat. Austin, Texas: University Art Museum, 1965.

1966 Freed, Eleanor. "Art." *The Houston Post,* May 15, 1966.

Freed, Eleanor. "Charles Schorre." *The Houston Post,* November 20, 1966.

"The Ninth Upland Game Bird." *Playboy,* November 1966.

Charles Shorre cover story. *Idea* (magazine of international advertising art in Japan) (not printed in English), 1966.

The 44th Annual of Advertising & Editorial Art. Hastings House.

1967 Stermer, Dugald. "Charles Schorre." *Communication Arts Magazine,* vol. 9, no. 2, 1967.

1968 White, Ralph. Foreword. In *Charles Schorre.* Exh. cat. Houston: DuBose Gallery, 1968.

1970 Kent, Norman. "Artists Studios." *American Artist,* January 1970.

Freed, Eleanor. "Ecology on Canvas." *The Houston Post,* November 1970.

1974 Moser, Charlotte. "From silkscreening to material collages." *The Houston Post,* January 27, 1974.

Bradym, Carlene. "Experiments In Color Collage." *The Daily Texan,* 1974.

1975 Stermer, Dugald. Review of *Drawings & Notes. Communication Arts Magazine,* vol. 17, no. 4, 1975.

1976 Crossley, Mimi. "Art: Charles Schorre at DuBose." *The Houston Post,* January 21, 1976.

Moser, Charlotte. "Schorre's Drawings Acutely Perceptive Work." *Houston Chronicle,* January 21, 1976.

Crossley, Mimi. "Art Notes." *The Houston Post,* March 7, 1976.

Moser, Charlotte. "Between Fantasy & Surrealism." *Art News,* May 1976.

"The Creative Process." *The Texas Architect,* May/June 1976.

1977 Scarborough, John. "Group at Cronin." *Houston Chronicle,* August 26, 1977.

Scarborough, John. "Group Show Has Work Not Seen Before at Photo Gallery." *Houston Chronicle,* August 26, 1977.

Moser, Charlotte. "The Joys of Color." *Houston Chronicle,* December 4, 1977.

1978 Moser, Charlotte. "Artist Charles Schorre has a finger in many pies." *Houston Chronicle,* November 29, 1978.

Glennie, Ian. Foreword. In *Charles Schorre: Recent Works.* Exh. cat. College Station, Texas: Texas A&M University, 1978.

Lacy, Bill N. Afterword. In *Charles Schorre: Recent Works.* Exh. cat. College Station, Texas: Texas A&M University, 1978.

Schiwetz, E. M. Essay. In *Charles Schorre: Recent Works.* Exh. cat. College Station, Texas: Texas A&M University, 1978.

1979 Lusk, Jennie. "Direction/Wildine Aims for Museum Quality in Inaugural Show." *Albuquerque Journal,* June 10, 1979.

Tennant, Donna. "Saudi Arabia/Schorre." *Houston Chronicle,* November 30, 1979.

Crossley, Mimi. "Art: In the Galleries." *The Houston Post,* December 2, 1979.

Curtis, Sandra J. "Texas Project." *Archives of American Art Journal/Smithsonian Institution,* vol. 19, no. 3, 1979.

1980 Moser, Charlotte. "But on the Other Hand." *Houston City Magazine,* February 1980.

Schjeldahl, Peter. "Art and Money in the City of Future Think: Some Artists." *Houston City Magazine,* February 1980.

Nelson, Mary Carroll. "Polarities and Parallels." *Artweek,* August 15, 1980.

Tucker, Marcia. "1980 New Orleans Triennial." Curator's statement.

1981 Crossley, Mimi. "Schorre: *Pages From Books Unpublished.*" *The Houston Post,* July 3, 1981.

Johnson, Patricia C. "'Pages' utilizes Schorre's interests in dual media." *Houston Chronicle,* July 3, 1981.

Kalil, Susie. "Charles Schorre at the Contemporary Arts Museum." *Art in America,* December 1981.

Cathcart, Linda, and Biff Henrich. "Charles Schorre: Pages From Books Unpublished." Curators' statement.

Chermayeff, Ivan. "A Commitment to Art." In *Pegasus on Creativity.* London: Mobil Corporation, 1981.

Owens, Don. "Charles Schorre: Saudi Arabia." *Photo Show, No. 4,* 1981.

1982 Cathcart, Linda L. *The Americans: The Collage.* Exh. cat. Houston: Contemporary Arts Museum, 1982.

1983 Everingham, Carol J. Review. *The Houston Post,* December 18, 1983.

Kalil, Susie. Afterword. In *Drawings & Notes II.* Houston: Seashore Press, 1983.

1984 Vander Lee, Jana. Review. *Artspace,* Spring 1984.

Johnson, Patricia C. "Schorre's Latest Work Remarkably Consistent." *Houston Chronicle,* November 12, 1984.

Helter, Steven, and David R. Brown. *AIGA Graphic Design USA 5.* New York: Watson-Guptil Publications, 1984.

1985 Johnson, Patricia C. Review. *Houston Chronicle,* January 19, 1985.

Johnson, Patricia C. Review. *Houston Chronicle,* January 25, 1985.

Communication Arts Magazine, no. 167, March/April 1985.

Crossley, David. "Charles Schorre's Artist's Handbook." *SPOT* (Houston Center for Photography), Summer 1985.

Rapier, April. "Photography in Houston." *Center Quarterly,* vol. 7, no. 1, Fall 1985.

Kalil, Susie, and Barbara Rose. *Fresh Paint.* Exh. cat. Austin, Texas: Museum of Fine Arts, Houston/Texas Monthly Press, 1985.

Nelson, Mary Carroll. *Layering.* Exh. cat. Albuquerque: Albuquerque, Museum, 1985.

1986 Johnson, Patricia C. "Art League Honors Schorre." *Houston Chronicle,* February 4, 1986.

"Mayor's Award Winners." *The Houston Post,* February 24, 1986.

Rapier, April. "Regionalism: A Sense of Place." *SPOT* (Houston Center for Photography), Fall 1986.

Johnson, Patricia C. "Three 'Slow, Difficult' Paintings Give Insight on Schorre's Skill." *Houston Chronicle,* November 12, 1986.

Olvey, Maggie. *The Photographic Print.* Exh. cat. Houston: Museum of Fine Arts, Houston, 1986.

1987 Webb, Nancy. "Charles Schorre: Letting Things Happen." *In Art,* March 1987.

Gambrell, Jamey. "Art Capital of the Third Coast." *Art in America,* April 1987.

Tucker, Anne. "Texas Dozen." *American Photographer,* April 1987.

Bell, James, and Lew Thomas. "To Remain in Doubt: An Interview with Charles Schorre." *SPOT* (Houston Center for Photography), Spring 1987.

Rapier, April. "Charles Schorre Outtakes." *SPOT* (Houston Center for Photography), Spring 1987.

1989 "The New York Art Review."

Chadwick, Susan. Review. *The Houston Post,* February 1989.

Vander Lee, Jana. Review. *The Houston Arts,* March 1989.

Birringer, Johannes. Review. *Public News,* May 17, 1989.

Chadwick, Susan. Review. *The Houston Post,* May 1989.

Johnson, Patricia C. Review. *Houston Chronicle,* May 1989.

Guild, Katherine. Review. *Houston Metropolitan,* June 1989.

Roberts, Anne H. "Beyond Permission." *SPOT* (Houston Center for Photography), Fall 1989.

1990 Fisher, James L. *Forty Texas Printmakers.* Exh. cat. for "Printmaking in Texas: the 1980's." Fort Worth, Texas: Modern Art Museum, 1990.

Vander Lee, Jana. "Painted Photography." *The Houston Arts.*

1991 Brauer, Deborah and David. "The Artist's Studio." *Cite,* Spring 1991.

1993 Johnson, Patricia C. Review. *The Austin Chronicle,* October 21, 1993.

Kalil, Susie. Review. *Houston Press,* November 25, 1993.

Publications by the Artist

Photograph series. *Popular Photography Annual,* 1957 and 1958.

Photograph series. *Creative Photography,* no. 3, 1959.

Cover. *American Artist,* November 1960.

"Top Drawer" (editorial). *Print,* 1962.

Sketches (with workshop members). Houston: Rice University, 1964.

Monograph #1. Houston: School of Architecture, Rice University, 1965.

"Art: In Churches, In the Kitchen." *Ramparts,* July 1966.

Cover. *News Front,* March 1967.

"Art Directing and Everything." *Ramparts,* April 1967.

Life Class. New York: Wittenborn, 1968.

Cover. For Raymond J. Nogar's *The Lord of the Absurd.* 1968.

Paintings. For Bishop James A. Pike's "The Other Side." *Look,* October 29 and November 12, 1968.

Editorial and cover. For Dr. Charles F. Jones's "Science & the Human Condition." *The Humble Way,* fourth quarter 1970.

Paintings and drawings. *Two Year Report.* Washington, D.C.: National Endowment for the Arts, 1972.

Artist's statement. *Who's Who in America,* 1974-1983.

Drawings & Notes. Houston: Seashore Press, 1975.

Paintings and drawings. *Picture,* vol. 1, no. 3, 1977.

Paintings and drawings. For William Caudill's *From Infancy to Infinity,* 1977.

Ten Figures, 1977.

Artist's Handbook series and exhibition options. *Picture,* vol. 1, no. 5, 1977.

Series of lithographs and etchings. Houston: Little Egypt Enterprises, 1978.

Drawings, writings, photography, and paint collages. *Picture,* vol. 1, no. 12, 1979.

Drawings & Notes II. Houston: Seashore Press, 1983.

Series of monographs. Houston: Little Egypt Enterprises, 1974.

Index

Works of Art Index

Artist's Handbook Index

Every effort has been made to correct-ly identify the persons shown. Our apologies if we have erred in any way.

Acknowledgments

The advisory board of the Charles Schorre Project came together in the summer of 1995 convinced that Mr. Schorre's quite remarkable body of work merited a broader audience. The concept of this book was explored and approved, as was the organization of a retrospective exhibition that would travel within Texas. An excellent tax-exempt fiscal sponsor, the Houston Artists Fund, was provided by our devoted C.P.A., Jody Blazek of Blazek & Vetterling LLP.

From the start, the project was blessed with a truly gifted editor, designer, and publisher, Jerry Herring, whose organization and associate, Laura Dignazio, have really made this publication possible. Our partners David Brauer, who organized the exhibition, and Jim Edwards, our principal writer, have contributed enormously to the success of our mission. Our readers who are familiar with quality arts publications will recognize immediately the superior photography of our generous partner Rick Gardner. We wish also to express our appreciation to William Otton, Director of the Art Museum of South Texas, the originating museum for the exhibition of Charles Schorre's work, who grasped immediately the lasting importance of Mr. Schorre's art. To Anne W. Tucker, Gus and Lyndall Wortham Curator at the Museum of Fine Arts, Houston, and to Geoff Winningham, distinguished photographer, we extend our thanks for their enlightened remarks about Mr. Schorre.

The formal launching of the project took place on October 25, 1995, when Elouise Cooper made her handsome restaurant available for a kickoff celebration and benefit. Since then literally hundreds of collectors and admirers of Charles Schorre's art and teaching have joined with corporate donors Mobil Corporation, PaineWebber, Inc., Rauscher Pierce Refsnes, Inc., and SBC Foundation to bring these projects to fruition. For all their support, we extend our grateful appreciation.

— Alexander K. McLanahan
Chairman, Charles Schorre Project

December 1, 1996

Contributors

For their support, we gratefully acknowledge Bob G. and Betty B. Agnew, Mr. and Mrs. William Akers, Marjory Yewer Alexander, Nancy C. Allen, Anchorage Foundation of Texas, Ben M. and Mary Anderson, Karen and Bob Anderson, Thomas G. and Martha A. Armstrong, Mr. and Mrs. C. E. Arney, Mr. and Mrs. William R. Aven, Ballard McDougal Burgher, Charles A. and Lelia D. Bankston, Barnes-Blackman Galleries, Kipp W. and Henry H. Baxter, Baxter + Korge, Inc., Tom and Dyanne Bean, Helen S. Bellhouse, Andrew Belschner, Dr. and Mrs. Bengt Bengtson, Julia Bering, Ellen T. Berman, Shane Berry, Eileen Biering and Nancy Biering Shoemette, Sarah Campbell Blaffer Foundation, Gay S. Block, John R. Blocker Sr., John and Jean Boehm, Dr. and Mrs. Ted Boone, Paul T. and Mary Jean Boston, Harvey J. and Margaret Deats Bott, W. J. Bowen Foundation, Jack and Sharon Boynton, Merle Bramlette, Lloyd and Jeannine Brandt, J. W. Branson Trust, Morris W. and Helen E. Brewer, Col. and Mrs. Robert O. Brewer, Richard L. and Robin Brooks, Donald D. and Kathy W. Brown, H. Fletcher and Katherine Tsanoff Brown, Mrs. Horace F. Brown Sr., The Rev. and Mrs. Fred Brown Jr., Jean William Brown, Mr. and Mrs. J. L. Brown Jr., Naomi H. Brown, Peter and Jill Brown, Joan K. Bruchas, William H. and Wendy Bruckner, Mr. and Mrs. B. M. Burgher.

We also thank Richard and Janet Caldwell, Bill and Jenny Camfield, Ralph S. and Lily G. Carrigan, John L. Carter, Janet M. Casperson, Dr. and Mrs. Francis Catlin, Penny Cerling, Russell L. Chaddick, Dr. and Mrs. Robert A. Chisholm, James B. and Joann W. Clapp, John Cleary Gallery, Martha S. Colangelo, Barbara Columbus, Patton Condren, Edward B. Cooper, Elouise A. Cooper, Jeffry Corbin, Gwen Rhea Cowden, H. Phillip Cowdin, Douglas S. Craig, Mary Louise Crain, Michael A. and Susan Crocker, Dorothy Daley, Dr. and Mrs. L. John Davis, Dominique de Menil, John and Betty Slaughter Dickson, Laurine W. Douglas, Wilfred S. and Sumarie L. Dowden, James Evans Dozier, Mr. and Mrs. Preston Dudley, Janet M. Duggan, Jeaneane B. Duncan, Mrs. Jane Dye, John and Linda Seaman Elford, Elkins Family 1983 Charitable Trust, Mineth and Grover Ellis, James A. and Jennifer Ann Embry, Clarence and Nancy K. Eriksen, Lunetta Erwin, Russell Erwin, Ted and Mary Eubanks, Jack and Lois Evans, C. Richard Everett, Jane Fair, The Favrot Fund, Carolyn P. Ferguson, Annie and Bob Flanders, Frederic and Betty Fleming, Joan H. Fleming, Stewart H. and Mary Boyd Folk, Mary Jane H. Forker, William C. Foster, Ralph and Martha Frede, The Jack Gaden Family, Jorge H. and Caroline B. Garcia,

The Garden Gate Company, Rick Gardner Photography and Mary Gardner, William P. Z. German III, Elisabeth B. Glaeske, Mr. and Mrs. Noel Gibbons, George and Margaret Gideon, Lester and Burdine Giese, Mrs. Clare Attwell Glassell, Jean and Hays Glover, Robin and Hays Glover and Family, Dolores and Mack Goble, Howard Greenberg, Charles and Jane Gregory, Dorothy Hackney, Mr. and Mrs. Frank J. Hafernick, Mr. and Mrs. Billy D. Hahn, Mr. and Mrs. G. Graham Hamilton, Jeffery C. and Janet Scott Harp, Mr. and Mrs. J. W. Henson, L. M. Hermes Jr., Herring Design (Jerry and Sandy Herring, Tom McNeff, Steve Freeman, Laura Dignazio, Debbie Moss, Matt Davis, Tracy Evans, and Doris Clark), Max H. and Isabell Herzstein, Lauren L. and Kathleen B. Hill, Mrs. Ray W. Hoagland, Mr. and Mrs. Elvis L. Hoffman, Nora and Ralph Howard, Robert E. and Rodella S. Howard, Richard Howe, Cynthia and Ellen Hoyt, Interfin Corporation, Betty B. Jackson and Family, Guy Jackson, John and Martha Jackson and Family, Mr. and Mrs. O. D. Jackson, Virginia Hartle Jackson, Betty Jones, Ann M. Judd.

We also thank the Joanne S. Julian Family, Robert Keith and Mette H. Julian, Jess Kaps, Marc S. and Bill Kemper, Emilie S. Kilgore, Karl and Kathy Kilian, Jonathan and Cynthia King, Ada Kirk, Mr. and Mrs. Howard W. Kleinecke, Dr. and Mrs. Riki Kobayashi, Frances and Joe Kurth, Robert and Andrea R. Lapsley, Mr. and Mrs. James P. Lee, Donna S. and Norman Lewis, Dr. and Mrs. W. R. Livesay, Clara Lock, Mr. and Mrs. Meredith J. Long, Dennis Lyall, Robert B. and Elaine S. Lynn, Douglas G. and Suzanne B. MacLean, Ronald L. and Mariana B. Madry, Dr. and Mrs. Pat Makins, Mr. and Mrs. Brownson Malach, Mary Malcik, Robert C. Mankin, Alexandra R. Marshall, Mr. and Mrs. Downs Matthews, Diane Mattly, Bill and Martha McCardell, Mary Fielding McCleary, Frank E. and Jacki McCreary III, Jerry and Molly Macon McHenry, Mr. and Mrs. Alexander K. McLanahan, Kathy McLean, Larry McMurtry, Herbert A. and Ava Jean Mears, Dr. and Mrs. Robert H. Meier III, Mel Anderson Communications Inc., Marcia Lacy Melin, Sol and Thelma Meltzer.

We also thank Carolyn E. Mitchell, George and Cynthia Woods Mitchell, Mitchell Energy & Development Corp., Frances Moore, Mr. and Mrs. James C. Morehead Jr., Helen S. Morgan, Joan Morgenstern, S. I. and Suzanne K. Morris, Dr. and Mrs. Donald Muller, Joe S. Mundy, John I. Mundy, Dr. Arthur Munford, Goldie S. Murphy, Doris Houck Nelson, Olive M. Neuhaus, Howard and Jan Nisbet, Kermit and Katie Oliver, Jane B. Owen, William and Jeanette Pakalka, John H. Parker, Alton and Laurel Parks, Betty Pecore, Karl A. and Jon S. Pelegrin, James L. and Kaylon Phillips, Rick and Nancy Pittman, Mr. and Mrs. James M. Pohlman, Sue and John Poretto, Sarah A. Post, Calvin and Patricia Powitzky Jr., Provident Enterprises, A. K. and B. E. Pruitt, Kathryn and Richard Rabinow, Eliza Lovett Randall, Harry S. and Frances C. Ransom, Ruth Raun, Macey Hodges Reasoner, Dr. Stanley J. and Katharyn D. Reiser, Mr. and Mrs. Raymond Reue, Mr. and Mrs. Howard Reynolds, Sally K. Reynolds, Michael W. and Teresa L. Risley, W. Stephen and Marci M. Rodgers, Betty and David Rolke, Virginia P. Rorschach, Dr. and Mrs. Thomas Rowe and Family, Craig M. and Jean B. Rowley, Janice Rubin, Jeffrey Ryan, Annette Sanford, Louisa Stude Sarofim, Judy Camp Sauer, Gwendolyn B. Scherz, Lee and Beth Schlanger, Mr. and Mrs. John M. Schmitt, Barth and Jane Schorre, Miggie Schorre, Marvin and Joan Schorre, Tim and Gail Schorre, Dr. R. Douglas Schultz, Dr. and Mrs. H. Irving Schweppe Jr., Evelyn White Shankle, Shannon Clinic, Mr. and Mrs. Frank B. Sheppard, Sierra Vista United Methodist Church, Mr. and Mrs. C. W. Silliman, Don M. and Marjorie M. Simechek.

We also thank Margaret C. Skidmore, Lomis and Marcia Slaughter, Mr. and Mrs. Lester Smith, Thomas C. and Mary Lu Smith, Ronald S. Spolane, Sharon D. Steen and Jary Dunnam, Dr. and Mrs. Alton L. Steiner, Dan R. and Donna A. Stewart, Linda Stone, Richard Stout, Frances Strauss, Dr. and Mrs. Dan Stultz and Family, C. Rex and Alice M. Stulz, Sara Stultz, W. K. and Gatha B. Symmes, Anne Allen Symonds, Today's Vision–Rice Village P.C., Anderson Todd, Lucie Wray Todd, Mrs. W. C. Tracy, Anne Tucker, Mr. and Mrs. C. Lee Tucker, W. Robert and Gertrude K. Vaden, Lissa and Paul R. Vahldiek Jr., Yvonne R. Victery, Mr. and Mrs. Ronald B. Walker, Dr. and Mrs. George L. Walmsley, Dr. and Mrs. G. Storm Walmsley and Thayer, Dr. and Mrs. Robert Phipps Walmsley and Andrew, Robert G. and Linda Thomas Ward, Judy King-Watson, Dr. J. Garland Watson Jr. and Laurie Quinn-Watson, Mary Johnston and W. Temple Webber III, Fay Weber, James and Marilyn Wennermark, Timothy T. and Catherine A. West, The Rev. Dr. and Mrs. G. Richard Wheatcroft, Mrs. J. Wheeler, Mr. and Mrs. Ralph White, Thomas E. and Madison H. Whitson, Lettalou G. Whittington, Judy Sublett Wild, Clinton T. Willour, Mr. and Mrs. Wallace S. Wilson, Mr. and Mrs. James E. Winn, Dorothy H. Winslett, Trish Witcher, Donald and Jill Wood, Paul and Valerie Woodcock, Dr. J. David Wright, Mr. and Mrs. R. P. Wright Jr., Eric and Caroline Zeringer and Family.

Charles Schorre
©1997 Herring Press

Published by Herring Press and
the Houston Artists Fund

Herring Press
1216 Hawthorne
Houston, Texas 77006
Phone: (713) 526-1250; Fax: (713) 526-1861
Email: jerryh@herringdesign.com
Web address: www.herringdesign.com

Houston Artists Fund
c/o Blazek & Vetterling LLP
3101 Richmond Avenue, Suite 220
Houston, Texas 77098

Produced by Jerry Herring and
Laura Dignazio

Edited and designed by Jerry Herring
Introduction by Anne Wilkes Tucker
Essay by Jim Edwards
Exhibition curated by David E. Brauer
Major photography by Rick Gardner
Additional text by Geoff Winningham, James
Bell and Lew Thomas, Ivan Chermayeff,
Dave Crossley, Carol Everingham, Norman
Kent, Patricia C. Johnson, and Dugald
Stermer.

Photography assistance by Mary Gardner,
proofreading by Polly Koch.
Printed in Hong Kong by Dai Nippon.

All photographs in this book are by Rick
Gardner, ©1997 Rick Gardner, with these
exceptions: Front cover of dust jacket,
©Greg Stephens; p. 2, ©Steve Brady;
pp. 3-4, 15, 17, 24(below), ©Jerry Herring;
pp. 7, 8, 10-11, 54-65, 69, 76, ©Charles Schorre;
p. 22(above), ©Gary Fay; pp. 42-43, ©Geoff
Winningham. Unfortunately, pp. 9, 19, 37,
unknown. All photographs shown in the
Charles Schorre work were taken by Schorre
and are ©Charles Schorre.

Special thanks are extended to Sandy Herring,
Steve Freeman, Tom McNeff, Matt Davis,
Doris Clark, Debbie Moss, Bonita Olson, and
Tracy Evans, as well as Sherry Adams, Doris
Anderson, Cecilia Burgin, Jean Caslin, Jean
Coyne, Michael G. DeVoll, Steve Douherty,
Carole Ann Hamel, Richard Hinson,
Fredericka Hunter, Lars Lerup, Meredith Long,
John Lunstroth, Misty Moye, Jan and Bill
Pakalka, Donald L. Pierce, Jeanette Pliner, Lana
Richards, Lori Shepard, Noboru Watanabe,
Cathy and Tim West, and Linda Wilhelm.

Every effort has been made to correctly identify the owners, sizes,
and media of the art shown. We also made great efforts to identify
photographs and rid the text of typographical errors. Our sincere
apologies if we have erred in any way.

Library of Congress Number 96-79770
ISBN 0-917001-13-3

Editorial Contributors

Herring Design is an eight-person graphic design firm in Houston, Texas. Established in 1973 — and a one-time tenant of Charles Schorre's at his Morningside studios — the firm has been widely acknowledged in national and international publications for its corporate and editorial design. In 1984, Jerry and Sandy Herring formed Herring Press, publishers of a range of visually oriented books, including *Santa Fe, Historic Galveston, AIA Guide to Houston,* and *Presence, The Transco Tower.*

Houston Artists Fund is a tax-exempt charity that serves as fiscal sponsor for art projects and organizations in the Houston area.

Ann Wilkes Tucker is the Gus and Lyndall Wortham Curator of Photography at The Museum of Fine Arts, Houston, where she has worked since 1976. She founded the Photography Department at the museum, which now has a collection of over 9,037 photographs. She has curated two dozen exhibitions including retrospectives for Robert Frank, Ray K. Metzker, George Krause, and Richard Misrach. A frequent lecturer throughout the U.S. and Europe, she has been awarded fellowships by the National Endowment for the Arts, the John Simon Guggenheim Memorial Foundation, and The Getty Center.

Jim Edwards is the Director of the Weil Gallery and Lecturer of Art at Texas A&M University–Corpus Christi. He was a Rockefeller Fellow in Museum Education and Community Studies in 1973-74 and was a Curator of Art at the Alaska State Museum, Juneau; the Boise Gallery of Art, Idaho; the Art Museum of South Texas, Corpus Christi, and the San Antonio Museum of Art. In 1985-87 he was Executive Director of the Victoria Regional Museum, Victoria, Texas. He has taught art history and criticism at the San Francisco Museum of Modern Art, California State University, Sonoma, and the University of Texas at San Antonio.

David E. Brauer teaches at the Glassell School, where he is currently Head of the Art History Department, at the University of Houston, Central Campus, and at the Women's Institute for Cultural Studies. Educated at the Sir Christopher Wren School, London, and the St. Martin's School of Art, London, Brauer has worked at the Museum of Modern Art, Oxford, and taught at Oxford Community College and North Oxfordshire College of Art & Technology in London. His guest lectures have included appearances at Columbia University, University of Notre Dame, University of Georgia, San Antonio Museum of Art, University of Texas at Austin, the Contemporary Arts Museum, Houston, the Menil Collection, Houston, and the World Business Council, Brussels, Belgium.

Rick Gardner is a photographer in Houston, Texas. A graduate of Rice University with a master's degree in architecture, Rick was enrolled in Charles Schorre's first "People, Cars and Trees" drawing class in 1961, which later became the "Life Drawing" class. After graduating, Rick opened a freelance photography business specializing in large format photography of architecture, interiors, and artwork. A tenant of Schorre's for 14 years and a frequent photographer for the artist, he brought his 25-year relationship with Schorre with him to this project.

Geoff Winningham is a widely published and exhibited photographer. He is the author of five books, including *Rites of Fall, Friday Night in the Coliseum,* and *Going Texan,* and a frequent contributor to *Texas Monthly* magazine. He is a Professor of Art at Rice University.

This publication and the forthcoming exhibition of Charles Schorre's work were not initiated as retrospective or memorial endeavors. Both were planned in celebration of Schorre's life as an artist. They remain so today.

Just days after Schorre's death, I returned to his studio. A note with my name scrawled across it designated the stack of drawings below for viewing. The artist's absence from his studio accentuated the peculiar sense of familiarity in all else. Everything remained the same since my last visit — pencils, paper, and paint out, that contrast still of Schorre's small, dense Rice Village studio with the wide open desert space of his imagery. But the emptiness of the studio now echoed the silence of those West Texas vistas he loved. Schorre once remarked that since his arrival in Houston during the late 1940s, the city's status of "visual wasteland" had contributed to his development as an artist. This wasteland, he said, turned him inwards, adding, "I would have had an awful boring time of it in Aspen, Colorado." Schorre looked everywhere, at everything, producing many works in many mediums and in many styles. All were indelibly his, from large, brilliantly colored paintings to terse, fluent drawings.

The polarities of Schorre's work, the body and the spirit, vast spaces and the enclosure of the studio, encompass the polarities of the artist. The central subject of *Pages From Books Unpublished* is an intense mediation and exploration of the possibilities inherent in the human figure, compared with other natural forms: shells, bones, etc. Drawings, watercolors, collages, oil paint. Endlessly inventive, Schorre could focus in on a breast, a hand, a patch of skin, and find an entire world. He could as fluently find in the vast space of West Texas or Saudi Arabia an intimacy. Other works address a sometimes explicit, and at other times a veiled, spirituality. All of the best work has a fierceness. Perhaps, like Caravaggists of the seventeenth century, Schorre found the body through the spirit and the spiritual in the smallest detail of the body.

With frequent disturbances from workmen at his house, Schorre had not done much painting in the last few weeks. While there was no "last" painting on the easel, there were his last triptychs, a favorite format for the artist and as similarly evocative of religious art as the Rothko Chapel.

Schorre's work conveys less a story than a web of associations: sometimes a person, perhaps an event, or especially a place. The place is often Texas, where Charles came from, and the artist embodied many of the mythic qualities of a Texan: tall, rangy, tough, quiet, laconic, full of humor, and possessed of "cool." Lawrence Durrell once characterized the artist as an aristocrat of the spirit. That fits Schorre just fine.

I first met Schorre in 1976, shortly after my arrival in Houston. Bob Camblin, Dave Folkman, Lucas and Patti Johnson, Charles Schorre, Don Shaw, Earl Staley, Dick Wray, and others met each Thursday at the Chaucer Bar, located in the basement of the Plaza Hotel on Montrose Boulevard. Schorre asked if he could take my photograph. We went outside and he shot me with my hands next to my face. I didn't know what he was doing, but I liked and trusted him immediately.

Most of these artists remained in Houston and taught at the old museum school on Garrett, St. Thomas University, the University of Houston, and Rice University. Schorre taught at Rice.

Some artists exert an influence by what they do, others by who and what they are. Schorre was, I think, of the latter persuasion. That is to say, his influence was in how he communicated the process of creativity, how he taught students and others to think for themselves. Stylistic influence is the most superficial of influences. The greater achievement is to teach by example how one may become a thinking, functioning, creative being. That is why Schorre exerted such an influence on so many people who were not artists. That is why so many of his friends needed to own his work — not as a token of loyalty but rather to have a living example of his method in their private lives. Creativity is, after all, a way of being, not just a way of doing. It has been, more often than one might have wished, a somewhat disappointing experience to meet an artist whose works one has admired. I never met anyone who was not glad to have known Charles Schorre. In him one was reminded of the rigor and discipline of being an artist. Up or down, ill or well, he went to his studio and worked. He did what all true artists do, ignoring the fluctuations of taste and market. He simply did the work.

— David E. Brauer

September 1996